Exploring England's Heritage

HERTFORDSHIRE TO NORFOLK

Judith Cligman and Nigel Crowe

Published in association with

English ✱ Heritage

London: HMSO

Judith Cligman worked for English Heritage as an Inspector of Historic Buildings until 1991 when she joined Essex County Council as a specialist adviser. She holds an MA in medieval architecture from the Courtauld Institute of Art and is a Council Member of the Ancient Monuments Society. As a pilot, she has gained a new perspective on the buildings and landscape of East Anglia.

Nigel Crowe worked for English Heritage in the 1980s, and is now the Heritage Manager for British Waterways. The life and works of the Norfolk architect Sir Roger Pratt formed the subject of his PhD thesis. He is currently writing a book on canal architecture, and in his spare time enjoys flying around East Anglia with the Cligmans.

Exploring England's Heritage
Other volumes already published in the series:

CUMBRIA TO NORTHUMBERLAND
John Weaver
ISBN 0 11 300029 4

DEVON AND CORNWALL
Andrew Saunders
ISBN 0 11 300025 1

DORSET TO GLOUCESTERSHIRE
Martin Robertson
ISBN 0 11 300028 6

LONDON
Elain Harwood and Andrew Saint
ISBN 0 11 300032 4

YORKSHIRE TO HUMBERSIDE
Jane Hatcher
ISBN 0 11 300026 X

British Library Cataloguing in Publication Data

A CIP catalogue record for this book is available from the British Library

While the information contained in this book is to the best of our knowledge correct at the time of publication, the publisher and authors can accept no responsibility for any inconvenience which may be sustained by any error or omission. Readers are also reminded to follow the Country Code when visiting the countryside monuments in this book.

The county names and boundaries used in this guide were correct at time of going to press, and are those used prior to the Local Government Commission review of 1993/4.

Front cover: Ely Cathedral, detail from painting by Thomas Lound. Norfolk Museums Service (Norwich Castle Museum).

Back cover: Woodbridge Tide Mill on the River Deben. Jarrold Publishing

Frontispiece: Lavenham Guildhall. John Bethell

HMSO publications are available from:

HMSO Publications Centre
(Mail, fax and telephone orders only)
PO Box 276, London SW8 5DT
Telephone orders 071-873 9090
General enquiries 071-873 0011
(queuing system in operation for both numbers)
Fax orders 071-873 8200

HMSO Bookshops
49 High Holborn, London WC1V 6HB
(counter service only)
071-873 0011   Fax 071-873 8200
258 Broad Street, Birmingham B1 2HE
021-643 3740   Fax 021-643 6510
33 Wine Street, Bristol BS1 2BQ
0272 264306   Fax 0272 294515
9–21 Princess Street, Manchester M60 8AS
061-834 7201   Fax 061-833 0634
16 Arthur Street, Belfast BT1 4GD
0232 238451   Fax 0232 235401
71 Lothian Road, Edinburgh EH3 9AZ
031-228 4181   Fax 031-229 2734

HMSO's Accredited Agents
(see Yellow Pages)

and through good booksellers

Printed in the UK for HMSO
Dd 294235   C60   4/94

Contents

Foreword

Today as midsummer approaches, Oxford is crammed with tourists. The roads near my office are choked with open-topped buses, their multilingual commentaries extolling the virtues of the city, while the pavements are impassable with crocodiles of visitors, eyes glued on the coloured umbrellas of determined guides. Dons wearing full academic dress attempt to make their way to and from the Examination Schools, to the delight of foreign photographers, and might as well be extras employed by the Tourist Board.

Oxford, Stratford-on-Avon and London together make up the golden triangle – golden, that is, to the tour operators – and millions of tourists are led through their crowded streets each year. The great majority of those who visit Oxford come for only a few hours, then move on to Stratford to stay overnight before returning to familiar London. It is London that takes the brunt. Westminster Abbey will be host to over 3 million, more than 2 million will visit the Tower of London, and then of course there are the museums and art galleries welcoming their annual tidal wave. Tourism, as governments are pleased to remind us, is one of Britain's biggest industries.

Looking at the tired, bewildered faces of the tourists off-loaded and scooped up again outside Oxford's St Giles, I long to grab them and say, 'It's all right – this is *not* what it's about. England is a beautiful, gentle country full of fascinating corners, breathtaking sights – an eclectic mix of unsurpassable quality. All you need is someone with vision to show you how to start looking.'

Well, people with vision, as well as the knowledge of our cultural heritage and the ability to communicate, are not in ample supply, but the members of the team assembled to write the eleven volumes of *Exploring England's Heritage* share these qualities in abundance. Each author has a detailed and expert involvement, not only with the region they are writing about, but also with the buildings, the earthworks, the streets and the landscapes they have chosen to introduce us to. These guides are no mere compilations of well-worn facts, but original accounts coloured by the enthusiasm of people who know what makes a particular site so special.

Each volume introduces more than 100 places. Some are well known (who would dare to omit Stonehenge or Hadrian's Wall?); others are small-scale and obscure but no less interesting for that. We are led down alley-ways to admire hidden gems of architecture, into churchyards to search for inscribed stones and along canals to wonder at the skills of our early engineers. And of course there are the castles, the great houses and their gardens and the churches and cathedrals that give England its very particular character.

Exploring England's Heritage does not swamp you in facts. What each author does is to say, 'Let me show you something you might not have seen and tell you why I find it so particularly interesting.' What more could the discerning traveller want?

Barry Cunliffe

Acknowledgements

We wish to acknowledge the help of all our colleagues at English Heritage and at Essex County Council. In particular we are grateful to Elain Harwood, Diane Kay, Martin Robertson, Richard Morrice and Pete Smith. Thanks are due to Philip Crummy, Jenny Glazebrook and Dave Buckley for their comments on chapter 1. Stephen Heywood kindly answered questions on Norfolk and Nick Roberts drew our attention to eastern England's public houses. We are also grateful to our editors Vanessa Brand and Ruth Bowden. Our partners Alison and Marshall deserve our greatest thanks for their encouragement and endurance.

Authors and publisher would like to thank the following for permission to reproduce illustrations: American Battle Monuments Commission, A F Kersting, Bedfordshire County Council, British Museum, Olive Cook for Edwin Smith's photographs, Stephen Croad of the National Monuments Record at RCHME, *Country Life*, Derek Pratt, David Perman of the Ware Society, Essex County Council, English Heritage, Foster Associates, Ipswich Borough Council Museums and Galleries, John Bethell, James Stevens Curl, Derek A Edwards, Ken Kirkwood, Norfolk Archaeological Unit, Norfolk Library and Information Service, Norfolk Museums Service, National Trust, P D Barkshire and Richard Rackham. We are also grateful to Essex County Council Planning Dept for permission to adapt the site plan for entry no. 5 from *Historic Towns in Essex*, Colchester: ECC, 1983.

Notes for the Reader

Each site entry in *Exploring England's Heritage* is numbered and may be located easily on the end-map, but it is recommended especially for the more remote sites that the visitor makes use of the relevant Ordnance Survey map in the Landranger series. The location details of the site entries include a six-figure National Grid reference, e.g., SX 888609. Ordnance Survey maps show the National Grid and the following 1:50,000 maps will be found useful: 131, 132, 133, 134, 142, 143, 144, 153, 154, 155, 156, 166, 167, 168, 169, 177 and 178.

Readers should be aware that while the great majority of properties and sites referred to in this handbook are normally open to the public on a regular basis, others are open only on a limited basis. A few are not open at all, and may only be viewed from the public thoroughfare. In these circumstances readers are reminded to respect the owners' privacy. The *access codes* which appear in the heading to each gazetteer entry are designed to indicate the level of public accessibility, and are explained below.

Access Codes

[A] site open for at least part of the year
[B] site open by appointment only
[C] site open by virtue of its use, e.g., a road, theatre, church or cinema
[D] site not open but may be seen from the public highway or footpath

Abbreviations

ABMC	American Battle Monuments Commission	JSC	James Stevens Curl
AFK	A F Kersting	KK/FA	Ken Kirkwood/Foster Associates
B	Bedfordshire	NAU	Norfolk Archaeological Unit
BCC	Bedfordshire County Council		
BM	British Museum	NC	Nigel Crowe
C	Cambridgeshire	NCC	Norfolk County Council
CL	*Country Life*	NLIS	Norfolk Library and Information Service
DP	Derek Pratt		
DPWS	David Perman, Ware Society	NMS	Norfolk Museums Service
E	Essex	NT	National Trust
ECC	Essex County Council	PDB	P D Barkshire
EH	English Heritage	RCHME	Royal Commission on the Historical Monuments of England
ES	Edwin Smith		
H	Hertfordshire		
IBCMG	Ipswich Borough Council Museums and Galleries	RR	Richard Rackham
		S	Suffolk
JB	John Bethell	SML	Stuart McLaren
JC	Judith Cligman		

Further Information

Further details on English Heritage, the Landmark Trust and the National Trust may be obtained from the following addresses:

English Heritage, PO Box 1BB, London W1A 1BB
Landmark Trust, 21 Dean's Yard, Westminster, London SW1P 3PA
National Trust, PO Box 39, Bromley, Kent BR1 1NH

Introduction

'Very flat, Norfolk', wrote Noel Coward. This elegant generalisation shall be our starting point to explore the rich diversity of the area of eastern England between the Thames and The Wash. There is no convenient name for our six counties, for they have never formed a single coherent region. 'East Anglia' is the best we can do, but whilst this label may be stretched to encompass Cambridgeshire and Essex, the counties of Bedfordshire and Hertfordshire sit uncomfortably under its umbrella. Historically a fluctuating threefold division can be detected, broadly identified with Norfolk and Suffolk, historic East Anglia, traditionally looking outwards to its North Sea connections, Essex and Hertfordshire focusing on London, and Cambridgeshire and Bedfordshire drawn always into the Midlands.

Over and above local variations, a number of common themes do emerge. The underlying geology, as always, determines the character of the landscape, the area's economy and to a great extent the man-made features within it. The lack of building stone in the region is a key factor. The north-west tip is just clipped by the limestone belt, running diagonally across country. There are pockets of older sandstones in the west, the lower greensand producing the hot 'gingerbread' carstone which outcrops around **King's Lynn** (94, N) and forming the hilly ridge which runs through Woburn. The only other notable local building 'stones' are the iron conglomerate 'puddingstone' and septaria, a concretionary clay. A wide swathe of chalk, containing rich flint seams, runs from St Albans (H) up to the north coast of Norfolk as far east as **Blakeney** (92, N), forming the so-called East Anglian Heights. Clay is the other dominant feature, found throughout the region, with a narrow strip of gault in the west and London clay across Essex, providing the raw materials for brick manufacture.

Large parts of this low-lying region lay under water, or in constant danger of flooding, for much of its history, and today the east coast continues to crumble into the sea. In the west it is pierced by the Chilterns, but even the chalk escarpment of the Dunstable Downs around Whipsnade, much frequented by hang gliders, only rises to 600 ft (183 m) above sea level. The East Anglian Heights rarely rise over a couple of hundred feet. But within this there is surprising variety. The coastal scenery is one of wide sandy beaches and shingle, besieged by the devouring North Sea which swallowed the medieval town of Dunwich (S). Muddy inlets and estuaries, like the Blackwater at Maldon, produce some of the least-spoilt scenery of the south-eastern corner. The gently undulating, prosperous pastoral landscape typified by the Constable country of the **Stour Valley** (101, E, S), the rolling chalk downlands around Newmarket and the uneventful Fens and marshland of Norfolk and Cambridgeshire are all aspects of the scenery. The drama is in the towering skies pierced by the towers of church and windmill, which form the enduring image of the region.

Man's impact on the landscape has been as great here as in any part of England. Settled early, and one of the most heavily populated areas in the Middle Ages, the region has been and continues to be transformed by the demands of agriculture. The Fens provided abundantly for the needs of its inhabitants from at least as early as the Neolithic period. During the 17th century the people of this isolated and marshy environment gained a fearsome reputation as the Fen Tigers. But they fought in vain to protect their ancient way of life from the Adventurers, drainage engineers and entrepreneurs who tamed the landscape into its present rigid form. Only at the National Trust's Wicken Fen (C) does the old landscape survive. The picturesque maze of water-

Nocturnal view of Ely Cathedral across the River Ouse. DP

Turf Fen windpump, Cambridgeshire. DP

west, particularly in Bedfordshire which, agriculturally, belonged to the Midlands, heartland of the open-field system. The Enclosure movement of the 18th century gave this area a planned landscape. In Norfolk, too, prosperous, corn growing estates were created from wasteland by the likes of Coke of Holkham and 'Turnip' Townsend.

The region owes its wealth primarily to agriculture and the industries which arose naturally from it, cloth manufacture, milling, malting and brewing. Grain production is reflected by the great timber and flint barns. Wool was exported even before the Conquest, and continued to make East Anglia hugely wealthy throughout the Middle Ages as its building stock eloquently expresses. The cloth producing areas, with some exceptions, suffered a long-term decline from the mid-16th century, to which is due the survival of medieval towns such as **Lavenham** (95, S). After the resurgence of Cambridgeshire and Norfolk during the Agricultural Revolution, the region faded gently into relative obscurity, lacking the mineral deposits and fast-running water which powered the Industrial Revolution.

London has long exerted its influence over the counties of Hertfordshire and Essex. The former is dissected by roads, railway lines and canals running north from the capital. From the 17th century Hertfordshire supplied water to the Metropolis via the New River. The prosperous commuter villages, typified

ways known as the Norfolk Broads was created by medieval peat extraction on a vast scale. Ancient woodlands of the heavy clay soils survive at Epping (E) and **Hatfield Forest** (85, E), but the once sandy open heath of Norfolk's Breckland has been transformed by pine plantations.

Before the rape of the countryside by 20th-century 'agribusiness' with its windswept prairies, Essex and the neighbouring parts of Hertfordshire and Suffolk were characterised by a complex patchwork of fields, divided by winding, high-banked lanes. These were the product of enclosure of fields at an early date, in some cases straight from the wild. It is a very different story in the

Paston Great Barn, Norfolk, one of the region's finest threshing barns, built of local flint and reed thatch. AFK

2

The Sun Inn, Saffron Walden, Essex. Medieval timber framing enriched by vigorous, rustic 17th-century pargeting. JB

by Much Hadham, have always been gentrified, and Georgian mansions mingle with lesser houses down the village streets. Suburbia now spills out into Watford (H). In Essex the reeking industrial Thames corridor, once one of the richest parts of the county feeding the capital's insatiable appetite for dairy produce, pork and poultry, gives way to grey, unrelenting suburbia before a whiff of fresh air is perceived beyond the M25. The pioneers of the Garden City Movement and the post-Second World War planners reacted against all this with the verdant Welwyn Garden City (H), **Letchworth** (96, H) and the brave 'New Town' of Harlow (E).

Colchester has a reasonable claim to the title of England's oldest town, built as it is on **Roman Colchester** (5, E), or Camulodunum. **Cambridge** (93, C) and

Norwich (97, N) are the foremost historic cities in the region. In Cambridge the ancient division of town and gown are poised in precarious balance, the bustle of the crowds threatening to gain ascendancy over the stillness of the academic cloister. To visit King's College Chapel, one of the wonders of the medieval world, as the crowds mill about, vacant eyed, can be a disheartening experience. In Norwich, commerce was ever king, although a combination of civic pride and piety left a remarkable legacy of medieval churches.

The smaller towns are compendiums of local materials, brick, flint and, above all, an abundance of handsome timber framing. Few areas have anything to compare with the wealth of East Anglia's timber buildings. It would be a mistake

to categorise the entire output as vernacular. The sophistication of design and opulence of materials of the medieval houses of the rich merchants and yeomanry of Essex and Suffolk is a world apart from the late mud-and-stud hovels of Bedfordshire. The whole traditional process of growing and conversion of timber for building was a highly organised and systematised operation which makes a fascinating field of inquiry of its own.

The lack of building stone had a profound effect on man's contribution from prehistoric times. There are none of the great stone circles or chambered tombs of the south-west, but equally remarkable in their way are the flint mines at **Grimes Graves** (4, N) and a timber lake village or ritual site at **Flag Fen** (3, C). The Romans produced brick

3

Early 16th-century decorative brickwork at West Stow Hall gatehouse, Suffolk. AFK

and concrete but their superior technology did not outlive their Empire. Saxon building was attuned to timber. After the Conquest only the most wealthy classes could afford to import stone, the Church for its greatest abbeys and cathedrals, royalty and the barons for their castles. The rebuilding of lesser churches in masonry, which had started before the Conquest, made sparing use of precious stone and turned to local materials of flint and timber, thatch, and later brick and tile.

The process of brick making in England was first revived in East Anglia, the richest region for the study of early brick buildings. Production was certainly under way by the 13th century. From the later 16th century the middle classes were impressing their neighbours by a show of tall and ornate brick chimney stacks, inserted into their timber open-hall houses. The chimney stack freed domestic planning, resulting in a dramatic improvement of living standards for the moderately well-off.

At higher social levels, grand timber houses began to be superseded by brick from the 15th century, with one or two notable earlier examples such as the 13th-century fortified house at Little Wenham (S). The great gatehouses of medieval **Oxburgh Hall** (17, N) and early Tudor **Layer Marney Towers** (83, E) gave way to the curly-gabled Artisan Mannerism of Raynham Hall (N). Brick was well suited to the lavish display of the Elizabethan and Jacobean prodigy houses and only the grandest, such as **Audley End** (75, E), then the largest house in the country, used stone. In the early 18th century even Lord Coke's lavish **Holkham Hall** (79, N) expressed its Palladian vision in white brick. Robust early Georgian houses generally favoured red brick, whilst the chaste white gault brick was much in vogue during the Regency. Mass production, started in the 19th century, dominates the Bedfordshire landscape with its sprawling brickfields and **Stewartby** (100, B) the London Brick Company town.

The organic relationship between the landscape and buildings began to be challenged by the transport revolution which made alien materials, such as

St Nicholas, Potter Heigham, Norfolk. A typical round-towered Norfolk church with flint walls and water-reed thatched roof. AFK

Welsh slate, cheaply available. Railways speeded up the pace of life and took over the ancient primacy of the waterways. Twentieth-century technology has given the region the steel and glass of the Foster Associates' buildings: the **Willis Corroon building** in Ipswich (73, S), the University of East Anglia in Norwich and **Stansted Airport** (71, E).

Our choice of buildings is unashamedly personal within our brief to illustrate many aspects of the rich history and character of our region. The emphasis is on buildings as history, not just as venerable antiquities or high architecture. We would have liked to have included more of the smaller private houses in which the region excels, but their interiors are hardly ever accessible to the public.

Most of all, we hope that the sites we have chosen will whet the appetite and lead on to further explorations of Hertfordshire to Norfolk.

1

Antiquities: Prehistoric, Roman and Pagan Saxon

'History' in our region starts only in the 1st century BC, from which time the Iron Age tribes of the Catuvellauni, Trinovantes and Iceni begin to emerge from the pages of Roman writers such as Caesar and Tacitus.

For the preceding millennia of human occupation the only evidence is what survives on, or under, the ground. Visible remains of the type of large structures such as causewayed camps and henges which were being built elsewhere by well organised and settled farming societies from the Neolithic period (c.4000–2000 BC) are scant. But this does not mean that they did not exist. Aerial photography has been particularly important in revealing sites because, due to the lack of stone for building and centuries of intensive agriculture, little has survived above ground in comparison with some other areas. As early as 1929, Wing-Commander Insall, a pioneer of aerial photography, discovered the wood henge at Arminghall (N), which preserved the traces of a series of great timber posts set up in a horseshoe formation. The traditional methods of excavation and relative dating by the Three Age System of Stone, Bronze and Iron Ages are being augmented by new technology and perceptions of prehistory are being constantly challenged. Everything is open to reinterpretation, but there is still little prospect that all the mystery will be dispelled, which is perhaps just as well, for the sites listed in this section are some of the most evocative, if the most fragmentary, in the area.

One site which has given up its mysteries is the flint mine at **Grimes Graves** (4, N). As recently as 1950, it was thought to date from 10,000 BC, but radio-carbon dating has revealed that its true period of use was from c.2100–1800 BC. Flint was one resource which this region had in plenty and it was of first importance to a pre-metal society.

A chance find, informed by some educated guesswork, led to the discovery of the unprecedented late-Bronze Age ritual site at **Flag Fen** (3, C) as recently as 1982. Dendrochronology, or tree-ring dating, is being used as a major tool in the investigation of the thousands of waterlogged timbers which have been disinterred. Depending on the condition of the sample, a very precise felling date can be obtained by this method. This site highlights the practice of ritual sacrifice of prestigious bronze implements by breaking and then depositing them into rivers and lakes, which seemed to come to prominence as the traditional barrow burial declines in the later Bronze Age.

The barrow was, however, a remarkably long-lived and widespread tradition. The Neolithic long barrow is rare in this region, but there is a good deal of evidence of the later types of round barrow, which became common in the Bronze Age and are often found clustered together, as at the Five Knolls on Dunstable Downs (B). The odd conical mounds of the Bartlow Hills (E) are a Romano-British example, and the ancient practice was alive and well in pagan 7th-century Suffolk, at **Sutton Hoo** (6, S).

The inundation of the Fens evident at Flag Fen is one example of the increasing pressure on land, which is associated with the period traditionally known as the Iron Age. The powerful tribal groups which emerged at this time of population growth needed to defend their territories and built hillforts in many parts of Britain. They are rare in eastern England. **Warham Camp** (9, N) on the coastal plain of north Norfolk is one of the best preserved. Other examples are found at Wandlebury Ring, on the Gog Magog Hills near Cambridge, and Maidens Bower, Dunstable (B).

By the middle of the 1st century BC, Caesar had established the frontier of the Roman Empire on the north coast of Gaul. His expedition to Britain in 54 BC

Sutton Hoo, excavation of the largest mound in 1939. BM

met with opposition from the chieftains of southern Britain under the leadership of Cassivellanus, chief of the Catuvellauni. After receiving the surrender of the Britons, Caesar withdrew, having extracted a promise of an annual tribute.

Between this time and the invasion of AD 43, the area of Cambridgeshire, Hertfordshire and Essex occupied by the Catuvellauni and Trinovantes extended their trading links with the Empire and appear to have upheld treaties with Rome. Settlements mainly took the form of farmsteads and villages, but larger settlements developed at **Verulamium** (St Albans, 8, H) and Camulodunum (**Roman Colchester**, 5, E). Both became Roman towns after the Conquest in recognition of the position they already held in the social and political organisation of the region. Camulodunum was a major port and centre of industry producing metalwork and ceramics and was defended by a series of dykes. Luxury goods, including amphorae of wine and olive oil, were imported. Rich burials have been found, such as the Lexden tumulus, over 72 ft (22 m) in diameter which contained, amongst other things, bronze figurines and a silver medallion of the Emperor Augustus.

The area of Norfolk and north Suffolk was dominated by the Iceni tribe, which after the Conquest initially managed to retain greater independence as a client kingdom to Rome. This arrangement came to a sudden and brutal end on the death of their king, Prasutagus (AD 60). The subsequent uprising led by his queen, Boudicca, took the occupying forces unawares. The rebels were crushed, but not before they had swept across the south-east, massacring Roman and British inhabitants alike, and leaving Camulodunum, Verulamium and Londinium burning in their wake. Within ten years the Romans had imposed a new tribal capital upon the Iceni at **Venta Icenorum** (7, N).

After this time the road network which underlies much of the present-day system began to be extended into Norfolk. The Peddars Way remains an impressive feature, cutting its way across the Norfolk and Suffolk

landscape. A great gravel causeway was constructed across the Fens from Castor near Peterborough (C) to Denver (N). Drainage canals, the Lode and Car Dykes, were cut at Reach (C) and Waterbeach (C) linking into a system of waterways.

From the 3rd century AD, Saxon incursions and pirate raids on the south-east coast of Britain led to the building of a chain of forts from the Solent to The Wash. **Burgh Castle** (1, N) is the best preserved in the region. There were others at Brancaster (N), Walton Castle near Felixstowe (S) and Bradwell-on-Sea (E).

East Anglia was, with Kent, the first region to be settled by Germanic immigrants, in the early 5th century. The traditional notion of the Anglo-Saxons overrunning England 'by fire and sword' is now given little credence. But the truth is that the period of migration and the formation of the kingdoms of East Anglia and Essex between the 5th and 7th centuries remains obscure. The **Devil's Dyke** (2, C) is a case in point. The date of its construction has never been established. Some believe it to be a British defence of the 5th century and others date it to the 6th to early 7th centuries, when the two emergent kingdoms of East Anglia and Mercia struggled for control over the territory of the Mid-Angles in the west of the region.

The Venerable Bede (c.673–735) is the most illuminating written source for the period. It is from his pages that the East Anglian King Raedwald (died c.625) springs, torn between the conflicting influences of Christianity and his proud pagan ancestry. The Sutton Hoo ship burial was Raedwald's cenotaph, an ostentatious assertion of the traditional values of a dynasty which claimed descent from Woden.

1

Burgh Castle, Norfolk
AD c.260

TG 474045. Burgh Castle, on minor road 3 miles (4.8 km) W of Great Yarmouth. Castle on footpath from church

[A] EH

Burgh Castle, the east wall of the fort. JC

Burgh Castle formed the penultimate link in a chain of Roman forts which spanned the coast of Britain from the Solent to The Wash. They were constructed from the late 2nd to the 4th century AD. By that time the Empire had reached its greatest extent and was under increasing pressure from barbarian attack. The Count of the Saxon Shore was appointed to guard the Channel and North Sea from Saxon pirates and to fend off the incursions along the coast. Burgh Castle, known as 'Gariannonum', was one of the forts in which he stationed his forces. It was built in a strategic location commanding a harbour at the mouth of the Yare Estuary, towards the end of the 3rd century.

Burgh is by far the most complete of the East Anglian forts. Brancaster (N), the most northerly, was dismantled in 1747. Only a fragment of wall survives at Bradwell-on-Sea (E) and Walton Castle near Felixstowe (S) has long since vanished beneath the waves.

A number of the forts were taken over by Saxon settlers and acquired important churches in the early years of their conversion to Christianity. Bede relates that in AD 633 King Sigeberht, son of Raedwald, gave Burgh Castle which was then known as Cnobheresburgh, to the Celtic missionary Fursey to build his monastery. The site of a timber church destroyed by the Danes has been traced in the south-west corner. Over it the Normans raised a motte which was in turn destroyed in 1839.

Gradually the estuary mouth became blocked by the development of the sandspit on which Great Yarmouth was built. The solitary fort now commands a wide expanse of marshland, punctuated by the towering forms of drainage windpumps. On three sides the walls stand to almost their full height, girded with big circular bastions, each of which carried a timber superstructure or a huge catapult called a *ballista*. In places, the neat split flint facing, banded with levelling courses of bricks, still adheres to the rubble core. On the west side the wall has fallen away and, where it was undermined by the deep ditch of the motte, one of the great bastions lies toppled like some Brobdingnagian chess-piece.

Devil's Dyke. RCHME

2

Devil's and Fleam Dykes, Cambridgeshire
?6th–early 7th century

Devil's Dyke TL 538555–TL 652585. Crosses A45 1½ miles (2.4 km) SW of Newmarket

[A]

Fleam Dyke TL 538555–TL 558532. Crosses A11 between Fulbourn and Balsham, 4½ miles (7.2 km) SE of Cambridge

[A]

In Cambridgeshire the prehistoric Icknield Way which linked East Anglia with Wessex is crossed by a series of gigantic linear earthworks which are amongst the most mysterious monuments in the region. Two of them, huge banks lined by deep ditches known as the Devil's and Fleam Dykes, are still imposing features in the open landscape. The Devil's Dyke, running from Reach (C) to Woodditton (C), would have made a formidable barrier across the open chalk downs between the impassable Fens and impenetrable forest, to forces advancing along the Icknield Way from the south-west.

Excavation has failed to reveal conclusively who built them and when. At Reach the Devil's Dyke meets up with the Lode, or Roman canal, which carried clunch from its quarries to the port of

Upware (C) on the River Cam. But the earth ramparts are certainly post-Roman. Under the Saxons this was border country, occupied by the Mid-Angles, but fought over by the two powerful rival kingdoms of Mercia and East Anglia. It was during their struggle for dominion that the dykes were most likely to have been thrown up. By the mid-7th century Mercia had swallowed Mid-Anglia and in 653–4 King Penda finally defeated East Anglia, killing King Sigeberht in battle.

A footpath, with a view of the racecourse, follows the summit of Devil's Dyke to Reach, whose medieval inhabitants flattened the end of the great earthwork to form their village green.

3

Flag Fen, Cambridgeshire
c.1000–800 BC

TL 227989. Signposted from Peterborough ring road A1139

[A]

Although it looks like nothing more than a lot of old wooden stumps embedded in a bog, Flag Fen is one of the most exciting English archaeological discoveries of recent years. In November 1982 the archaeologist Francis Pryor came across a protruding oak stump disturbed by a digger cleaning out the medieval Mustdyke, close to where it is

crossed by the Roman Fen Causeway just outside Peterborough. Clues to its significance were the way in which it had been hacked to form a post and that it emerged from 3.25 ft (1 m) below the level of the Roman road.

Excavation on the site revealed thousands of timbers, perfectly preserved by immersion in the acidic waterlogged peat. They composed part of a platform estimated to be about the size of two football pitches with the remains of buildings upon it, which had been built out in the shallow waters of the Fen in the late Bronze Age. Before the great drainage works of the 17th century, this had been a wild and watery landscape, but one which the 12th-century writer Hugh Candidus recorded offered an 'abundance [of] all things needful for them that dwell nearby'. People had settled on the Fen edge since at least Neolithic times (*c.*4000–2000 BC).

Pryor's next major discovery, in 1989, concerned a structure of posts running for over ½ mile (0.8 km) in length across and beyond the platform. At first he thought it could be a causeway linking the platform with dry land, but it became apparent that it had been constructed after the platform had been abandoned because of rising water levels, perhaps as some kind of barrier. On the seaward side was unearthed a remarkable collection of metal artefacts, which included swords, daggers, helmets, tools and delicate items of

Flag Fen excavations, some of the thousands of timbers which made up the platforms and buildings upon them. EH

Other late-Bronze Age sites have revealed similar evidence. It seems to relate to the placing of rich grave goods in barrow burials, leading Pryor to suggest that 'we are seeing here symbolic, if not actual burial of important people in the waters'. The wide range of objects suggest a complex ceremonial, a public display of wealth and prestige, votive offerings, perhaps even propitiation of the power of the sea itself, which threatened to inundate the Fen edge communities.

Modern drainage of the Fens has reduced the ground level in places by as much as 13 ft (3.9 m) in the last 100 years. Drying out is a severe threat to Flag Fen, so a lake has been formed over part of the site, to preserve the unexcavated part of the platform which lies beneath it. Those who brave the unattractive approach road through Peterborough's Eastern Industrial Estate are rewarded by a guided tour of excavations in progress and a permanent display of the remarkable finds and prehistory of the area in a new timber visitors' centre built out on the lake.

4

Grimes Graves, Norfolk
c.2100–1800 BC

TL 818898. 3 miles (4.8 km) NE of Brandon signposted from B1108

[A] EH

The strange, pitted lunar landscape of Grimes Graves was once barren Breckland heath, but is now enclosed by dark pine plantations. Its mysterious craters were, like other inexplicable earthworks, ascribed to Grim, or Woden, by the Anglo-Saxons, whose word 'graves' simply means holes or hollows. In 1739 the Norfolk historian Blomefield came up with an ingenious theory that the site was 'a very curious Danish encampment . . . The pits are dug so deep and are so numerous that they are capable of not only receiving a very great army, but also of covering it from the eyes of passers by.' This imaginative vision is dispelled by the true explanation, discovered by the

bronze jewellery. Pryor believes that they had been deliberately broken and deposited in the water as part of an

elaborate ritual. Curiously, this ancient practice has echoes today in the custom of dropping coins into a fountain.

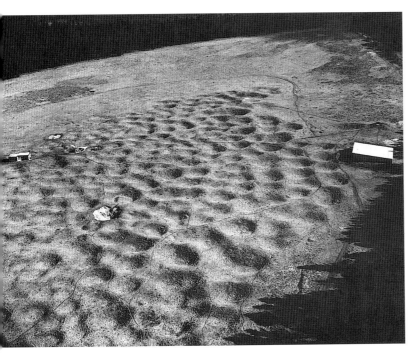

Grimes Graves from the air. NAU

celebrated amateur archaeologist Canon Greenwell in 1870. Greenwell dug out one of the hollows to find that it was in fact a backfilled mineshaft.

In this part of Norfolk an underlying bed of chalk contains rich seams of flint. These were a valuable source of tools before the advent of metalworking, as flint can be split, flaked and polished to form a very sharp edge. The seams are of variable quality and to reach the finest black 'floorstone' it was necessary on the higher ground to sink shafts, some reaching a depth of around 40 ft (12.1 m). There are over 700 such shafts, only a few of which have been excavated, in addition to shallower pits in the 34 acres (13.7 ha) in English Heritage guardianship, which is less than half of the total area of the mines. Visitors can descend by fixed ladder into one of the capped shafts from the bottom of which radiate the entrances to seven back-achingly low galleries running off to link with other shafts.

Radio-carbon dating has established that the main period of mining was from the late Neolithic to early Bronze Age, c.2100–1800 BC, during which the

deeper shafts were dug. Less intensive open-cast mining continued around the northern and western edges until around 1600 BC, by which time flint was no longer in such demand. To dig the deepest shafts, it has been estimated that it would have taken twenty men between eighty to 100 days, using over 100 picks made from the antlers of red deer as well as stone or flint adzes. Wooden ladders were probably used to carry the flint to the surface where the nodules were roughly formed into axes, knives and other tools on site. Water transport could then have been used to distribute them throughout the region, or even further afield.

5

Roman Colchester, Essex
AD c.1st–2nd century

TL 998254. Colchester town centre and Castle Museum

The name Camulodunum, 'the fort of Camulos the war god', evokes an image of a barbarian stronghold in the

benighted regions beyond the Roman Empire. But by the time of the Roman invasion in AD 43, the great Catuvellauni settlement in the annexed territory of the Trinovantes was a town in the making. It occupied an area of about 12 sq miles (31 sq km) between the Colne and Roman rivers defended by a system of dykes, impressive sections of which can still be seen in the Lexden and Stanway areas (E). It was already a flourishing port trading with the Empire, and its mint struck coins in the name of Cunobelin (Shakespeare's Cymbeline), who died *c.* AD 40.

The Romans seemed to have viewed it as the 'capital' of southern Britain. Immediately after the invasion, a legionary fortress was established on the hilltop to the east of the main settlement, into which the Emperor Claudius made a triumphal entry. In AD 49, after the withdrawal of the garrison, it was made a chartered town, or *colonia*, the first of the kind in Britain, for veteran legionaries who held the status of Roman citizens.

Amongst the first buildings to be erected was the Temple of Claudius, the centre of the Imperial cult, which was intended to be the religious focus for the entire province. This massive classical temple raised up on a high podium, was clearly designed to overawe the natives. But it does not seem to have achieved the desired result, for according to Tacitus it so incensed the Trinovantes that they enthusiastically joined Boudicca's revolt, razing the infant town to the ground in AD 60. Ironically, it was here that the citizens made their last desperate stand. Remarkably, the vaulted concrete podium survives, built into the foundations of a later symbol of Imperialist domination, the Norman castle.

Other public buildings already erected before the rebellion were the council chamber and a theatre. Just north of the present High Street, the burnt-out remains of a fully stocked pottery and glassware shop were found. The finest of over a hundred excavated mosaics and tessellated pavements are on display in the Castle Museum.

The Roman walls, which contained the expansion of the town until the

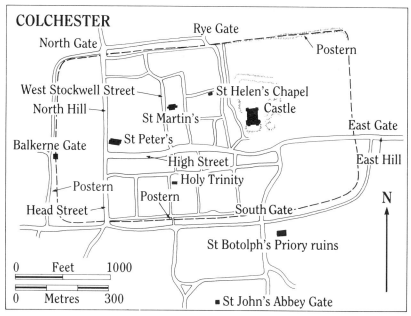

COLCHESTER

North Gate
Rye Gate
Postern
West Stockwell Street
St Helen's Chapel
North Hill
Castle
St Martin's
East Gate
St Peter's
Balkerne Gate
High Street
East Hill
Holy Trinity
Postern
Postern
N
Head Street
South Gate
St Botolph's Priory ruins

0 Feet 1000
0 Metres 300

St John's Abbey Gate

Colchester town centre, showing the line of the Roman wall (after ECC). EH

beginning of the last century, have recently been redated to the immediate post-rebellion period, making them much the earliest major Roman defensive walls in England. In the absence of a more suitable building stone, septaria, with brick levelling courses, was used. With medieval additions, the walls remained more or less intact until the siege of 1648. The core still survives over most of the circuit, with substantial sections up to 13 ft (3.9 m) high, but crumbly and overgrown in places. The monumental, battered Balkerne Gate, which defended the London road entrance on the west side, is the largest surviving Roman gate in England.

6

Sutton Hoo, Suffolk
Saxon: probably early 7th century

TM 289486. Near Woodbridge, A12(T) from Ipswich. Signposted footpath ½ mile (0.8 km) W of B1083

[A] Guided tours weekend afternoons in summer months only

Beowulf, the Anglo-Saxon epic poem, written down in about the year AD 700, describes the ship burial of the Danish King Scyld. The tomb of the hero Beowulf himself was not a ship but 'a barrow on a headland, it was high and broad, visible from afar to all sea farers'. The Saxon royal barrow cemetery at Sutton Hoo presents a striking parallel to the poem. Here, to glorify another great warrior, a huge ship was hauled up onto the escarpment above the Deben Estuary, lowered into a trench and buried beneath a mound of earth. This was the most magnificent burial to have survived at the eighteen-mound site. Others have revealed the traces of a second ship and the double grave of a young man and his horse.

Today an effort of the imagination is required to appreciate the original impact of this remote and windswept site. The coastline has changed, a wood has grown up to block the view of the river and the barrows have been eroded away. However, the outline of the ship marked on the largest of the mounds gives an idea of its prodigious size, nearly 90 ft (27.4 m) long and 14 ft (4.2 m) in the beam. Remarkably, the exact impression of the clinker-built

ship, with each of its iron rivets still in position, was preserved in the sandy soil to be discovered during the excavation of 1939. Under the remains of a timber roof amidships lay a collection of magnificent grave goods, but no human remains were found. It was hoped that the mystery of the missing body would be solved when the mound was reopened in 1967, but this was not to be, and more recent investigations have revealed very variable survival of human remains throughout the site.

The Sutton Hoo helmet, even in its reconstructed state, forms a powerful icon of the age. It is now on display in the British Museum with the rest of the grave goods which provided for all eventualities in the afterlife. The gorgeous jewels are amongst the best preserved items, like the great gold belt buckle with intricate interlaced beasts, similar in style to ornaments found in Swedish boat burials, and the shoulder clasps delicately inlaid with garnets and millefiore glass. The only ship burials to have been discovered in England are at Sutton Hoo and nearby Snape (S). Both lay within the territory of the Wuffinga dynasty, rulers of East Anglia from the late 6th century. The practice of the ritual of boat burial was one aspect of the common pagan ancestry of North Sea peoples.

Dating has relied heavily on the grave goods. The most likely recipient of the honour of the foremost ship burial was Raedwald, who died in about AD 625, the Wuffingas' most successful king. According to Bede, he established himself as Bretwalda or overlord of the Anglo-Saxon kingdoms by holding at bay the nascent power of the rival kingdom of Mercia. Although converted to Christianity by his ally, King Ethelbert of Kent, Raedwald soon reverted to pagan practices, setting up in the same temple altars 'to Christ and another to offer victims to devils'. Recently excavated human remains confirm the practice of ritual killings at Sutton Hoo. Against this background, the highly ostentatious ship burial emerges as a defiant reassertion of pagan traditions in the face of a new religion and a potent symbol of the successes and aspirations of a dynasty.

7

Venta Icenorum, Norfolk
AD c.1st–3rd century

TG 230035. Caistor St Edmund, 1½ miles (2.4 km) south of Norwich, between A140 and B1332. Next to church of St Edmund

[A] Norfolk Archaeological Trust

We had not defeated this powerful tribe in battle, since they had voluntarily become our allies.' Tacitus AD 47.

Boadicea, the warrior queen with the flashing knives at the wheels of her chariot, is a powerful figure of popular legend, a patriotic British heroine battling against the forces of tyranny. Boudicca, the historical figure, was queen of the tribe known to Caesar as the Cenimagni, or great Iceni. This powerful and wealthy tribe, which held the area of Norfolk and north Suffolk, had in the first decade of Roman rule kept its independence as a client kingdom. But this arrangement came to a bitter and violent end on the death of King Prasutagus. Tacitus relates how his 'kingdom and household alike were plundered like prizes of war', and his wife and daughters were no exception. These 'outrages and the fear of worse . . . moved the Iceni to arms.' The red-headed queen with 'an appearance almost terrifying' led her people to war, in an uprising which shook the newest colony to its foundations, with indescribable slaughter. But after the sack of Verulamium, the rebels were checked by the legions at an unknown battle site. Tacitus cautiously recorded that, according to some reports, 80,000 rebels died. Boudicca took her own life.

The uprising is dated to AD 60 or 61. The town at Venta Icenorum was laid out in around AD 70. There had been no previous Iceni settlement here. On the contrary, their tribal capital was probably in the Thetford (N) area. So it seems that the new Roman capital was imposed on the decimated tribe, on a site quite deliberately divorced from their traditional powerbase, calculated to avoid a nationalist resurgence.

Aerial photographs have revealed the town's grid plan and the footprints of the few public buildings of stone, the forum, basilica and baths with two temples standing side by side. Excavations have

Venta Icenorum, aerial photograph of 1928, showing the ramparts and grid plan of the town and the traces of the quadrangular forum near the centre. RCHME

given insights into the lives of the townspeople, living in timber houses, making pottery, glass and woollen cloth. Defensive ramparts topped by massive flint walls 11 ft (3.3 m) thick, which still stand to a height of 19 ft (5.7 m) in places, were not constructed until the 3rd century. By then the town had shrunk, or perhaps the layout had been too ambitious at the start, for part of the grid was excluded. Venta must have been one of the first towns to have fallen to the East Angles in the early 5th century, but in their time the regional capital migrated north to Norwich. Only the parish church of St Edmund is left standing within the walls, and this peaceful site evokes the desolate memory of the downfall of a once proud and valiant tribe.

8

Verulamium Theatre, St Albans, Hertfordshire
AD c.150–300

TQ 135074. St Albans, to west side of A414. From car park off St Michaels Street, adjacent to Museum

[A]

Verulamium Theatre, the excavations of 1939. RCHME

The Roman city of Verulamium lies buried beneath a public park on the edge of St Albans. The medieval town took its lead from the abbey, which forsook the site of the ancient town, preferring to commemorate the place of martyrdom of its citizen St Alban on the nearby hillside. The memory of the city's former glory was never entirely lost, for as early as the 10th century Abbot Ealdred 'searched through the ancient subterranean crypts of the ancient city which was called Werlamcestre . . . for they were hiding places of robbers, body snatchers and evil women and brought together a great quantity of stones, tiles and timber for the building of his church.' Despoilation continued apace, a major source of building material for the abbey and town.

During the 16th century antiquarians and poets alike took a more benevolent and romantic interest in the ruins which inspired Edmund Spenser's

Ruines of Time. William Camden, antiquary to Henry VIII, recorded the 'ruins of walls, chequered pavements, and Roman coins now and then digg'd up there'. In 1721 the eminent antiquary and archaeologist William Stukeley made an influential conjectural plan and the first archaeological excavation of 1847 produced the spectacular discovery of the Theatre. The comprehensive excavations of the town during the 1930s by Sir Mortimer Wheeler are documented in the Museum, which houses a remarkable range of artefacts, including wall-paintings and superb mosaics. Apart from the Theatre and sections of the city walls, there are few visible remains *in situ*.

Verulamium was founded in AD 49 as the administrative centre for the Catuvellauni tribe on the site of their existing stronghold of Verlamion. It was one of the few towns in Britain to have defences as early as the 1st century, but was nevertheless sacked by Boudicca in AD 60. Rebuilding commenced soon afterwards on the original grid plan.

The Theatre stood next to the Temple and was probably used not only for the performance of plays and other, more

savage, entertainments but also as a venue for religious and public festivals. Built about the middle of the 2nd century AD, it was well adapted to these various functions, being, in its original form, more like an amphitheatre than a classical semi-circular theatre. The almost circular arena with a small stage was surrounded by tiers of wooden seating on earth banks, which have been partly reinstated. Timber staircases on the outside of the retaining walls gave access to the seats whilst the performers emerged from vaulted tunnels beneath them.

Before the end of the 2nd century in a move towards greater sophistication, the Theatre was altered to bring it closer in form to a classical theatre, one of only three found in Britain. The stage now became much more important. It was enlarged and given a proper classical proscenium, or screen of Corinthian columns, one of which has been reinstated for effect. It seems to have reached its heyday in around AD 300 when it was enlarged to about 190 ft (57.9 m) in diameter by the construction of a new external wall to make room for additional seating. The rise of Christianity and the consequent suppression of buildings associated with pagan cults was probably the reason for its demise, and by the end of the 4th century it had been relegated to a rubbish dump.

9

Warham Camp, Norfolk
1st century BC

TF 943408. 3 miles (4.8 km) SE of Wells-next-the-Sea, off lane between Warham St Mary and Wighton

[A]

A quiet, deserted Iron Age camp, standing amidst fields and close-hedged lanes, Warham was a 'fort' or a 'defended farmstead', built in about the 1st century BC. A place of refuge, occupied perhaps only in emergencies by farmers and herdsmen, it is a circular enclosure covering 3.4 acres (1.4 ha) and protected by a pair of steep ramparts with ditches. Entrance to the camp was probably on the south-west side, where the walls were destroyed in the 18th century by the diversion of the little River Stiffkey. Three other gaps in the ramparts are relatively modern.

Defended camps were a feature of Iron Age England. Each was a response to local circumstances and there are regional variations. Other examples on the Norfolk coastal plain include Holkham, South Creake and Narborough. Warham, the best preserved, is fairly small, but must have

Warham Camp from the air. NAU

involved considerable skill and motivation to build. Excavations in 1959 revealed evidence of a timber palisade and fighting platform on top of the inner rampart. Originally the ditches were deeper and the ramparts taller; serious obstacles for attackers.

The grassy enclosure within the ramparts may have contained circular, thatched, timber houses and barns, but there is no clear evidence of this and it may simply have been used to protect grain-pits and to shelter livestock during troubled times.

Outside the camp there would perhaps have been other huts and small groups of fields cleared for cultivation of crops. But little is known of life in Iron Age Norfolk. Warham is archaeology that keeps the visitor guessing. It is also pleasantly lonely. Small, chalk-loving flowers and butterflies speckle the grassed-over ramparts with colour. Drowsy cattle take up 18th-century poses beneath gnarled trees. A good place to spend a summer's afternoon with a copy of Sir Thomas Browne's Norfolk-inspired *Urne-Buriall*.

Castles and Fortifications

The three eastern counties of the region were for centuries in the front line against invasion and are rich in coastal defences, the earliest of which are the Roman shore forts such as Burgh Castle (1, N). They also boast some of the finest and best preserved castles in England, which they owe to the last great military invasion, the Norman Conquest.

A contemporary chronicler of the Conquest wrote that although the English were warlike and courageous, they had been too weak to withstand their enemies because 'the fortresses which the Gauls call castella had been very few in the English provinces'. The type of fortification new to England that the Normans introduced was the motte and bailey castle with its tower or keep, an essentially defensive structure concentrated on an impregnable stronghold, which could be built with speed and defended by relatively few men.

William the Conqueror moved quickly to tighten his hold on his new domain, prompting the *Anglo-Saxon Chronicle* to complain, in 1067, that the invaders 'wrought castles widely throughout the nation and oppressed the poor people'. William caused castles to be built in all the county towns of the region, of which there are only fragmentary remains at Bedford, Cambridge and Hertford. **Colchester** (12, E) was singled out for the dubious honour of the largest masonry keep in Europe. Timber buildings were the norm in the early years, often replaced by more substantial structures during the following century. Norwich (97, N) only received its ornate stone keep (refaced in 1834 by Salvin) in the reign of Henry I.

The Norman aristocracy followed the king's example, building castles on their newly acquired estates. William de Warenne's late 11th-century Castle Acre (N) took the form of a pair of first-floor halls within a defended enclosure, which may reflect a Saxon type. The turbulent reign of Stephen saw the building of a number of fully-fledged stone keep and bailey castles. The de Vere Earls of Oxford, major landowners in Essex and Suffolk, built **Castle Hedingham** (10, E), perhaps the finest tower keep in the country. William de Albini's **Castle Rising** (11, N) took a lower, rectangular form, closer to the fortified first-floor hall type. The Albinis also built the circular shell keep of New Buckenham (N), probably mid-13th century and the earliest of its kind in England.

At a lower social level the first-floor hall was adopted for fortified manor houses. Little Wenham Hall (S; not open to the public) is an exquisite example of the late 13th-century use of locally made brick. At **Longthorpe** (14, C) a tower combining privacy, comfort and defence was added to an earlier house in the 14th century, which gives a rare insight into the medieval interior.

At **Orford** (16, S) in the 1160s Henry II found it necessary to build a castle on a new site to counteract the power of the troublesome East Anglian magnates. Chief amongst these was Hugh Bigod, Earl of Norfolk. The king had confiscated Bigod's four strongholds in 1157, returning **Framlingham** (13, S) only upon payment of a large fine which helped pay for his new castle. Henry's precautions were rewarded, enabling him to crush the Bigod-led rebellion of 1173–4. Framlingham paid the penalty and was demolished, but was later rebuilt in revolutionary form. It was one of the first English castles of curtain wall type, whereby the defences were concentrated on a strong circuit of walls defended at regular intervals by protruding towers and a redoubtable gatehouse. It survives as the most romantic of castles, with its many towered silhouette.

The stone keep towering over town and countryside was as much a symbol of domination as a military device. It formed the centre of local administration and was a grand lordly

Orford Castle keep. AFK

residence, developing all the trappings of comfort and convenience. The architectural vocabulary of the castle, steeped in connotations of prestige and power, long outlived its military function. The great gatehouse with its crenellations and the moat remained a potent symbol into the Elizabethan period in private houses and collegiate institutions.

Caister Castle (N), built in brick for Sir John Fastolf in *c*.1435, and occupied by the Pastons from 1459–1599, was amongst the last true castles. One of the famous Paston letters records that it fell to a siege in 1469: 'The place is badly broken down by the guns of the other party, so that, unless they have hasty help, they are likely to lose both their lives and the place.' But domestic convenience and show were by then coming to outweigh military considerations. The next step in the process is seen at **Oxburgh Hall** (17, N) of 1482, one step away from the Tudor mansion, a courtyard house with a gatehouse dressed up in military clothing with a fine sense of the picturesque.

By the mid-16th century the castle as combined fortress and residence was obsolete. A 'Certificate of His Majesties decayed Castells' of 1609 includes both Colchester and Norwich, and many lesser structures had already long since fallen into utter ruin. Some, like Colchester, enjoyed a brief moment of glory during the Civil War, before being 'slighted', or ruined, by Cromwell's forces.

Town walls built by the Romans have already been mentioned. Those at Colchester (5, E) were repaired by the Saxons in the 10th century and again during the medieval period. Other towns acquired theirs at that time, including Great Yarmouth (N) and Norwich, both of which have impressive remains. The Civil War produced a string of hastily built earthworks around towns like Cambridge (93, C), Colchester and Norwich at a time when the eastern counties of England were 'the hotbed of Puritanism'. The Bulwark at Earith (C) is a rare survival of the period.

Castle Rising stairway. EH

Castle Hedingham Castle, the Great Hall. Engraving by J Burnett, from *Architectural Antiquities of Great Britain*, 1810. RCHME

The defence of the realm had relied on three things from the 16th century, a standing army, coastal defences and the Royal Navy. The 'wooden walls of England' backed by the coastal forts of **Tilbury** (18, E) and Languard Fort, Felixstowe (S) first built by Henry VIII, deterred aggressors. Those lonely sentinels, the Napoleonic **Martello Towers** (15, S), never saw action.

10

Castle Hedingham Castle, Essex
12th century

TL 788359. Castle Hedingham, 6 miles (9.6 km) SW of Sudbury, signposted from A604

[A]

Castle Hedingham is the archetypal *donjon*, or keep, with its massive, tall, square, stern silhouette. It is also perhaps the best preserved of all English tower keeps. Aubrey de Vere built it in around 1140, after he was made Lord Great Chamberlain during the troubled reign of King Stephen. His son, Aubrey,

was one of Queen Matilda's closest supporters, and she made him 1st Earl of Oxford. Matilda is said to have ended her days at Hedingham in 1151. The de Veres had, at the Conquest, been granted extensive lands in Essex, Suffolk and Cambridgeshire and were amongst the most powerful families in Norman England. Their emblems of the mullet (star) and the blue boar adorn many a church and public house throughout this area. The castle passed out of their hands only in the 17th century, when it was sold to Sir William Ashhurst, sometime Lord Mayor of London, who built the elegant house in the eastern outer bailey, preserving the keep as a somewhat overgrown garden ornament.

The keep, which rises to nearly 100 ft (30.4 m), was built on an enhanced natural eminence, dominating the surrounding countryside. The pretty town lies at its feet clustered around the parish church of St Nicholas with its Romanesque fabric and fabulous timber roof. It does not appear to have been enclosed by the western outer bailey, of which only a short stretch survives. The inner bailey, approached by a handsome late 15th-century brick bridge, enclosed not only the keep but a separate great hall and chapel which have vanished without trace. From a splayed base, the keep walls rise like a sheer cliff face. The battlements have gone, but the angles are fortified by clasping buttresses rising into square turrets.

The keep is divided into three floors above the basement, with fireplaces and private chambers with garderobes contrived within the thickness of the walls. The lofty hall on the second floor, encircled by a mural gallery, is spanned by a mighty arch. In quality and elaboration the masonry is exceptional, with fine mouldings and rich chevron arches both inside and out. Clad in costly Barnack limestone, the keep was the ultimate expression of the power and wealth of the de Veres.

11

Castle Rising Castle, Norfolk
12th century

TF 665246. In the centre of Castle Rising, off A149, 4 miles (6.4 km) NE of King's Lynn

[A] EH

The Albini name does not bear the familiar ring of the other great East Anglian dynasties the Mowbrays, Bigods or de Veres. But this is due to the early failure of their line after the death of the 5th Earl of Sussex in 1243. In their day they were unsurpassed among the Anglo-Norman aristocracy – and this day had arrived in 1138 when William de Albini married the Queen of England, Alice of Louvain, widow of Henry I and aunt to King Stephen.

This brilliant alliance brought William the earldom of Lincoln and initiated a lavish building programme. He chose Rising as the site for a resplendent new castle. To accommodate it he relocated the village to the north with a fine new parish church, leaving the old church stranded within the huge earth banks of the inner bailey.

Castle Rising is a 'hall' keep, a rectangular block, with the emphasis on width rather than height. There are two principal storeys over a basement, divided into unequal halves by a

Castle Rising keep. EH

structural cross-wall running lengthwise. The Great Hall and Chamber, kitchen and chapel are all on the first floor, reached from a staircase in the entrance forebuilding.

In the extent of architectural embellishment, it is second only to Norwich, and is surely a conscious attempt to rival the royal castle. The decoration is concentrated on the forebuilding which is lavishly embellished with interlaced arcading, chevron and billet mouldings, roundels and big shafted round-arched windows to the entrance vestibule. The experience of entering the keep remains impressive; a majestic flight of steps rises to the spacious vestibule and the grand shafted and richly carved archway into the hall, now blocked by a Tudor fireplace.

The roof and internal floors have gone, but the impression of a cold and comfortless fortress is misleading. The walls were plastered and painted (traces of the red chevron decoration on the chapel vaults survive) and hung with rich fabrics. There were fireplaces and two pairs of garderobes for hall and chamber housed in the thickness of the walls.

By 1243 when Rising passed into the hands of the Montalt family, the castle had already seen its heyday. During their ownership, the castle fell into disrepair. Between 1331 and 1358 Rising was once again home to a dowager queen, this time Isabella, 'the She-Wolf of France', wife of Edward II, whose downfall she had orchestrated. Thereafter her son, Edward III, granted the castle to the Duchy of Cornwall and it became part of the vast estates of the Black Prince. By the 1540s, when Henry VIII granted it to the Howards, a survey reported that 'the Castell of Rysynge and dyvers houses and walls within and aboute the same bene at this daye in great ruin and decaye', but fortunately the keep stood long enough for 19th-century antiquarian enthusiasm to ensure its survival.

12

Colchester Castle, Essex
11th century

TL 999254. Colchester High Street [A]

At Colchester in 1074–6 William the Conqueror ordered the building of a huge stone keep, bigger than his White Tower of London, and the largest in Europe. Masonry fortifications were very much the exception to the rule in the immediate post-Conquest period. Clearly there was a pressing need for William to impose his hold on his new territory in eastern England and to fend off the threat of Danish attack on the east coast. Colchester was an obvious focus. Its Roman walls and gates and remains of many of its buildings were still standing in testimony to its illustrious past. In 917 Edward the Elder had expelled the Danes and repaired the defences. By the end of the 10th century it had regained a mint and was reborn as a town.

The entire strength of the castle lay at first in its keep, for it was not raised on a high motte, and does not seem to have acquired its ramparts until around 1100 when the High Street was diverted to accommodate them. Instead, it was erected upon the vaulted concrete podium of the great Roman Temple of Claudius. It was raised in stages, reaching a height of about 80 ft (24.3 m). Built, like the Roman walls, from septaria, Roman bricks were reclaimed by the thousand to level courses of rubble and to turn arches and vaults. The occasional hypocaust pile was also incorporated *en bloc* into the walling, revealed by the stripping off of the facing which has exposed the rubble core.

Like the White Tower, the castle is a hall keep, and has an apsidal chapel, only the vaulted undercroft of which survives complete, and which projects in a great bulge from the side wall. The

Framlingham Castle from the west. Engraving by Samuel and Nathaniel Buck, 1738. SML

unusual entrance position on the ground floor, originally protected by a forebuilding, was an early 12th-century modification. The Great Stair still winds upwards; garderobes and big fireplaces, which sent their smoke out through louvres, survive in the thick walls. But the top stage, one of the two principal internal cross-walls and the main floors have been destroyed.

From the start the castle was held by royal gift, frequently by the County Sheriff. As its military role waned so its grisly reputation as a prison grew; Catholics were burned there in 1557 and in 1656 poor James Parnell, a Quaker youth, died after confinement in a hole 'called the Oven'. The top storey was dismantled in 1683, but total demolition was averted when in 1751 it came into the hands of Charles Gray, antiquarian owner of Hollytrees House, who adorned his gargantuan folly with a little domed turret. The cruel gaol was only closed in 1835 and became a museum in 1860, but it was not until the 1930s that the

empty shell was completely roofed in. The Romantic rugged remains depicted by Constable and Turner now rise incongruously from the manicured flowerbeds of a public park.

13

Framlingham Castle, Suffolk
12th–18th century

TM 287637. Framlingham, 19 miles (30.5 km) NE of Ipswich at junction of B1119 and B1116

[A] EH

From a distance Framlingham is a fairytale castle, a many towered ring of walls on a hill, rising from a shimmering mere. Its jagged, embattled outline is capped by spiral ornamental stacks added in the 16th century by the Howards with a keen sense of the picturesque. At closer quarters, the steep, smooth, grassy banks of the dry moat plunge away from the sheer walls, spanned by the single arch of a bridge. The grassy open court within, bereft of its baronial halls, lodgings and chapel, is now a place of quiet repose.

In *c*.1190 Roger Bigod built on the site of his grandfather's timber motte and bailey castle, which had been updated by his father Hugh, but demolished as punishment for leading the uprising against Henry II in 1173. Earl Roger adopted an innovatory form of military planning – the curtain wall fortification defended by protruding towers and a strong gatehouse. One of the earliest English examples of the

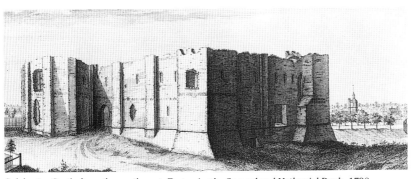

Colchester Castle from the north-east. Engraving by Samuel and Nathaniel Buck, 1738.

type, it took its lead from Henry's mighty castle at Dover. The keep was no longer the focus of defences, allowing the buildings to be disposed at will around the walls. The masonry walls form only the inner ring of defences within the earthwork enclosures of the outer bailey and lower court.

Roger's rebellious family managed to hang onto the castle until the failure of their line in the early 14th century, although it had been besieged and captured by King John's mercenaries during the Civil War in 1215. Thereafter the castle had a chequered history of regular forfeiture to the Crown, passing through the hands of both the Mowbray and Howard Dukes of Norfolk. It had a governor until 1572, but by then had lost all military significance. During Elizabeth's reign it was used as a prison for recusant priests. But in 1635 it was sold to Sir Robert Hitcham, who in his will directed that 'all the Castle, saving the stone building, be pulled down.' The Great Hall was converted to a poorhouse, which was rebuilt in 1729 except for the present custodian's house.

Below the castle lies the town, a pleasant huddle of buildings focused on the church, one of the best in the county. Its superb hammerbeam roof sports fan coving like the church of St Peter Mancroft in Norwich and the gracious east end was enlarged in the 16th century to house the Howard tombs, a supreme collection of Renaissance monuments.

Longthorpe Tower, east wall showing the Wheel of the Senses. EH

14

Longthorpe Tower, Peterborough, Cambridgeshire
14th century

TL 163983. 2 miles (3.2 km) W of Peterborough on A47

[A] EH

Robert de Thorpe, Steward of Peterborough Abbey, added a three-storey tower to his hall-house in around 1300–10. It was raised over a vaulted storage undercroft unconnected with the upper levels inside, like a real castle.

The two upper rooms, supplied with a fireplace and garderobe, gave Robert a new-found privacy and comfort to which he could withdraw from his rowdy retainers in the hall below. Apart from these advantages, the tower offered security and the obvious connotations of prestige. This was all important to a man who was only released from villein service in 1323 when he was confirmed in the influential post he had held since 1310.

What makes Longthorpe really exciting is the almost complete scheme of wall-paintings in the vaulted first-floor great chamber, which has been described by David Park as 'the major surviving monument of medieval secular wall painting in England, and one of the most impressive north of the Alps'. Medieval domestic wall-paintings are extremely rare and these are of exceptional quality. They were discovered under many coats of limewash in 1945 after the Home Guard had vacated the building.

The main theme of the paintings appears to be the contrast between the worldly and the spiritual life. They combine biblical subjects, including the Nativity and Apostles Creed, with moral allegories like the Three Living and the

Three Dead and the popular cycles of the Labours of the Months and the Ages of Man. Heraldry and marginal decoration in the form of naturalistic birds as well as the fabulous beasts of the medieval bestiary, such as the nasty Bonnacon, are equally prominent, as they are in contemporary manuscripts like those produced at Peterborough Abbey. Much rarer is The Wheel of the Five Senses above the fireplace. In this scene Reason in the form of a king is shown to rule over the physical senses represented by a monkey, a vulture, spider's web, boar and cook, symbolising taste, smell, touch, hearing and sight. The only similar known version of this theme in wall-painting form is in a Cistercian abbey near Rome.

The brilliant pigments have faded, but Longthorpe is the place for a rare glimpse of the splendours of the medieval interior.

15

Martello Towers, Suffolk
19th century

TM 366426 and TM 356397. On the coast between Shingle Street and Bawdsey

[D]

Martello towers, along with HMS Victory, Trafalgar and 'Boney was a Warrior', belong to English folk-memory of the Napoleonic Wars. In 1803 the French Grand Army was just across the Channel. Invasion scare was at its height. Rapid plans were made to improve England's beach defences by building a chain of 143 gun-towers between Littlehampton in Sussex and Great Yarmouth (N). Twenty-seven east coast towers were built between 1808 and 1812 and the system included a larger casemate redoubt at Harwich (E) armed with ten guns.

Inspiration came from a circular gun-tower at Cape Mortella, Corsica, which had beaten off a British naval squadron in 1794. The East Anglian Martello towers were of a similar design but oval in plan. They were built of brick 13 ft (3.9 m) thick at the base and 6 ft (1.8 m) thick at the parapet.

Four Martellos stand in a line, ½ mile (0.8 km) apart, between Shingle Street and Bawdsey on the deserted Suffolk coast. Spare, unadorned drums in a landscape of flat fields, distant trees and sea, their sculptural qualities are best seen close up. Towers Y and Z have crumbled like old cheeses, their brickwork rimed with salt and grey lichen. Towers AA and W are lived in.

The towers built on the east coast are bigger than those on the south coast. Dimensions varied although the design was standardised: thick walls punctuated by small rusticated windows like keyholes; doorways at first-floor level, reached only by ladder. Inside, a basement contained magazines and stores and the first floor provided accommodation for twenty-six men. A staircase in the wall led up to the roof, which mounted three guns. Their purpose was to fire upon ship-borne invaders and defend the beach until reinforcements arrived.

None of the Martellos saw action. By the time the chain was complete the Grand Army had gone away to Russia. Some of the empty towers were demolished or found new uses at a later date. Others were abandoned to time, chance and weather, and left as romantic objects by the seashore.

Shingle Street, the northernmost Martello Tower. RR

16

Orford Castle, Suffolk
12th century

TM 419499. Orford, 11 miles (17.6 km) E of Woodbridge on B1084

[A] EH

Orford is the first English castle for which documentary evidence exists. The Pipe Rolls, the annual records of the Exchequer, show that it was built for King Henry II in 1165–73 at a total cost of £1,413.9s.2d. This represented a huge sum, exceeding all of Henry's other castle works, except for Dover. At that time Orford had yet to be cut off from the sea by the spit of land known as Orford Ness and was still a major port. It was of great strategic importance to Henry, for it gave him control of the coastline in an area where the power of the barons was, at the start of his reign in 1154, unchallenged by the presence of a royal stronghold. Two rival magnates, Hugh Bigod, Earl of Norfolk and William of Blois, son of King Stephen, posed a serious threat to Henry. In 1157 he grasped the nettle, confiscating from them the castles of Bungay (S), Framlingham (13, S), Thetford (N), Castle Acre (20, N), Eye (S) and Norwich (97, N). In 1165 he returned Framlingham and Bungay to Bigod on payment of the massive fine of £1,000, but commenced his new castle at Orford the very same year. His mistrust of the earl proved only too well founded, and Orford Castle played an important role in putting down the Bigod-led rebellion of 1173.

Held for the king by a royal constable, the castle was a military base, the centre of local government and a powerful symbol of royal authority. The unique polygonal form of the keep with its three projecting turrets is a highly sophisticated design. It combines ingenious planning with symbolic overtones which rendered the fortress a grand royal residence of considerable comfort and convenience. It is the most fascinating of castles to explore.

At ground level, reached only from inside, is the basement with its well.

chapel above, and the impressive main stairs. Both halls have wide fireplaces and are lit by large windows. Around the walls of the lofty upper hall is a ring of corbels which originally supported the timbers of a conical roof. Boarded internally, this may have formed a high-domed ceiling to this grand apartment. This feature has been likened to the domed circular throne room, a Byzantine model resonant with the image of divine kingship, which Henry's designers may have consciously evoked to his greater glory.

17

Oxburgh Hall, Norfolk
15th and 19th century

TF 742012. At Oxborough, 7 miles (11.2 km) SW of Swaffham on Stoke Ferry Road

[A] NT

Oxburgh represents the final flowering of the Englishman's home as his castle, in a form which retained any semblance of a defensive purpose. The right to build a fortified house, for which a 'Licence to Crenellate' was required from the mid-13th century, was always just as much a matter of the symbolic display of status as of practical considerations. By the late 15th century, the heyday of the ornate brick gatehouse, the romantic associations of the castellated style were strong and Oxburgh is self-consciously picturesque.

Licence to crenellate was granted by Edward IV in 1482 to Sir Edmund Bedingfeld who erected the seven-storey red brick gatehouse with four domestic ranges around a courtyard, enclosed by a moat. The well-proportioned gatehouse is a relatively restrained example of the genre, the decoration being limited to graduated panels of brickwork with cusped corbels. The finely moulded entrance arch leads to a passageway vaulted in panels with heraldic bosses. Above are two fine rooms known as the King's Room and the Queen's Room, after the visit of Henry VII in 1487. They are linked by a circular vaulted newel stair, a virtuoso piece of brickwork,

Orford Castle, interior of the Great Hall. Reconstruction by Alan Sorrell. EH

Above are two circular halls. The private chambers, the chapel and kitchens are all housed in the towers, radiating off from the main rooms and reached by wall passages. This clever solution avoided the need to subdivide the main spaces with partition walls or to restrict the chambers to the wall thickness as had been the rule before. The private rooms are concentrated in the north tower where they could benefit from the

heat from the rear of the main stack. The 'constable's chamber' has its own urinal. The main garderobes are accommodated within the wall on the west side, next to the kitchens, thus concentrating foul drainage in one area. The kitchens have hearths, sinks and drains and on the top floor of the turret is a cistern which provided a water supply for their use. The south turret houses the entrance vestibule, with the

Oxburgh Hall from the north. AFK

paralleled at Faulkbourne Hall (E) and at Moot Hall in Maldon (E).

A priest's hole formed from a garderobe off the king's chamber is a reminder that the Bedingfelds were one of the principal recusant families, Catholics subject to persecution during the 16th and 17th centuries and prohibited from holding public office. Alterations to Oxburgh carried out in the 18th century included the demolition of the great hall and kitchen which formed the south range opposite the gatehouse. It was not until after the family's fortunes revived with Catholic emancipation during the early years of the 19th century that wholesale restoration and remodelling began.

A W N Pugin, Catholic architect and advocate of the Gothic Revival, described Oxburgh in 1831 as 'one of the noblest specimens of domestic architecture of the 15th century'. Another Catholic architect, J C Buckler, was employed to carry out extensive restoration between 1830 and 1870 for the 6th and 7th baronets. All the terracotta details, including the ornate stacks, windows, corbel tables and an oriel window are his. Buckler also added the south-east tower containing a suite of neo-Tudor rooms. The interiors of the west and north wings are a supreme example of oppressive High Victorian taste.

The chantry chapel, founded by Edmund Bedingfeld in the nearby church, was the place of burial of most of the family until the late 18th century. It contains two stupendous fantastical Early Renaissance terracotta screens erected around 1530, similar to those in the church at Layer Marney Towers (83, E), the Marneys and the Bedingfelds being connected by marriage.

18
Tilbury Fort, Essex
17th century

TQ 651754. SE of Tilbury

[A] EH

From the air Tilbury Fort is a star surrounded by water. From the ground it is a series of low, indistinct lines rising out of the Thames mud. It is England's best example of a bastioned Dutch-type fort.

Tilbury was an important strategic site for the defence of London. Between here and Gravesend on the other side, the Thames is only ½ mile (0.8 km) wide, and could be easily guarded by cannon. Henry VIII built the first fort in 1540. Elizabeth I, waving a small sword, made a fine speech here during the Armada crisis. That was the point: if an enemy got past Tilbury, then London was in trouble. In 1660 Charles II began to reorganise England's defences.

Tilbury Fort, the Water Gate. EH

Bernard de Gomme, a reliable Royalist, was put in charge. He became 'Engineer of all the King's Castles etc in England and Wales.' Plymouth Citadel was his first big job. At the same time he made three designs for a new Tilbury Fort, all of which were turned down. The Dutch Raid on the Medway in 1667 led to a rapid re-think and a final design of de Gomme's fort was adopted and built c.1670–85.

The old fort of Henry VIII was swept away and replaced by something simpler. Four arrow-head bastions were built. Five were intended but the riverside one proved too difficult. A double moat, ravelin and outworks provided defence in depth. Within the walls a large parade ground, guardhouse cum chapel, stores, barracks and magazines were created. The buildings were plain red brick with stone dressings. A single blaze of architectural glory was conferred by the Water Gate, a triumphal arch, loaded with stone trophies and classical ornaments, like the frontispiece to some 17th-century treatise on fortifications. 'A right Royal work indeed!' wrote the patriotic diarist John Evelyn.

Tilbury Fort was typical of the very best 17th-century west European military architecture. The Frenchman Vauban was the most brilliant exponent of the bastion system and de Gomme was nicknamed 'England's Vau' in acknowledgement of his own ingenious but derivative abilities. Portsmouth, Plymouth and Hull were similarly fortified under de Gomme's supervision but the work was not as severe nor as convincing as at Tilbury.

For much of Tilbury Fort's existence it was neglected. Life there was always dull and monotonous. Officers lived away in Gravesend if they could. Other ranks had to put up with the cold, uninviting conditions. Occasionally social events were held. One of these was a Kent v. Essex cricket match played on the parade ground in 1776. At some point in the game tempers flared, the umpire was ignored, players broke into the guardroom and armed themselves. In the ensuing battle several people were killed, others injured. It was the only real action Tilbury Fort ever saw.

3

Cathedrals and Abbeys

The Benedictines established themselves in the region at an early date and ensured their domination with a number of well-entrenched and powerful abbeys. **Ely** (21, C), **Peterborough** (23, C) and **St Edmundsbury** (25, S) were all Benedictine foundations of the 7th century, which were destroyed by the Danes but refounded during the 10th-century monastic revival. **St Albans** (24, H) had even earlier origins in a shrine of the late Roman period. During the 12th century large numbers of Augustinian houses were founded, St Botolph, Colchester (E) being perhaps the earliest. But, with the exception of the royal foundation of Waltham Abbey (E), they did not compare in sheer scale and grandeur with the Benedictine institutions.

By the time of the Norman Conquest the diocese of East Anglia (Norfolk and Suffolk) was centred on North Elmham (N). The ruins there purported to be the remains of the Saxon cathedral are now believed to be a late 11th-century bishop's chapel. Essex and Hertfordshire formed part of the diocese of London. For a brief period in the 7th century Cedd was bishop of the East Saxons and the chapel at Bradwell-on-Sea (44, E) was perhaps his cathedral. The rest of the region owed its allegiance to the fluctuating Midlands dioceses.

Although the half-Norman Edward the Confessor had previously rebuilt Westminster Abbey in Romanesque style, it was the Conquest which, as in military planning, ensured that the new style gained so rapid and thorough a hold in England. The monk chronicler, William of Malmesbury (c. 1090–c. 1143), described how, 'With their arrival the Normans breathed new life into religious standards, which everywhere in England had been declining, so that now you may see in every village, town and city churches and monasteries rising in a new style of architecture.'

In almost every case, the appointment of a Norman bishop or abbot heralded the rebuilding of a church in Romanesque style on a huge scale. Rebuilding almost invariably commenced at the east end so that the important business of worship could begin as soon as possible. St Albans, started in the 1070s, is one of the best examples of the earliest generation of Romanesque work in England. The rebuilding of Ely by Abbot Simeon, a kinsman of William the Conqueror, was begun in 1083 and it was raised to cathedral status in 1109. Peterborough had to wait until after a fire in 1116 for its first Norman Abbot, Thorold, had to contend with the depredations of Hereward the Wake, whose men twice sacked the abbey leaving it impoverished and in disrepair. The East Anglian diocese was transferred from North Elmham to Thetford (N) and finally to **Norwich** (22, N) where the new monastic cathedral was begun in 1096.

Peterborough and Norwich both still convey a good impression of the grand Anglo-Norman Romanesque church. It was typified by a plan comprising an apsidal choir, divided from the spacious nave by a monumental screen or pulpitum, with transepts and a crossing tower. On this plan rise three storeys of arcade, tall gallery and clerestory. The very early transepts of St Albans, which incorporate Saxon-looking baluster shafts, do not follow the standard formula. But this is a highly individual building, for the use of Roman brick imposed upon it a severe rectilinearity which was alien to the English love of decorative elaboration. At Ely, Norwich and Peterborough the plastic possibilities of the thick wall construction were exploited by the multiplication of shafts and mouldings in the 12th-century work.

Normandy was not the sole source of English Romanesque. The Norman twin-towered west end found no favour in East Anglia. Something grander and much more monumental was required to front these vast naves. St

Peterborough Cathedral, west front. JB

St Edmundsbury, the Great Churchyard and Church of St Mary. JC

Edmundsbury, and later Ely, adopted the wide screen facade with a large central tower. These massive 'west works' were Germanic in conception. Peterborough's celebrated west front is a peculiarly English hybrid, which owes a debt to Lincoln.

Subsequent alterations everywhere followed a similar pattern. Enlargement of the east end and the addition of a Lady Chapel accompanied the 13th-century enthusiasm for pilgrimage and the cult of relics, and a growing emphasis on devotion to the Virgin Mary. Rebuilding after fire or collapse was a fairly frequent occurrence, accounting for Ely's Octagon (one of the greatest feats of medieval carpentry and design) and the vaulting of Norwich in stone. Fashion was another powerful motive. Just as the baronial castle was an expression of status, so too were the great cathedrals and abbeys, which were a power in the land.

Many of the abbey churches survived the Dissolution of the Monasteries in the 1530s. Peterborough was raised to cathedral status whilst both Ely and Norwich remained cathedrals served by secular canons instead of monks. St Albans did not become a cathedral until 1877, but the church remained partially

in use by the town. St Edmundsbury was not so fortunate and only the rubble core of the abbey church survives to give an inkling of its once mighty stature. But at Bury St Edmunds, as well as Norwich, Peterborough and Ely, the close or monastery precinct still broods over the town.

The naves of many abbey churches were in parochial use and thereby survived the Dissolution, such as **Binham Priory** (19, N) and the dramatic Wymondham (N) with its two towers. Others stand completely in ruins, Cluniac **Castle Acre Priory** (20, N) being the most impressive. **Horsham St Faith** (26, N), like many smaller priories, was partly converted to a residence and a fine scheme of wall-paintings survives in the old refectory. The famous flushwork gatehouses of the Augustinian Butley (S) and St Osyth's (E) also became houses. The great preaching church of the Blackfriars at Norwich became a civic hall, ensuring its survival as the most complete friars' church in the country.

The 1541 edict that 'all Relics, Images, Table Monuments of Miracles and Shrines be demolished' had a

profound effect on the appearance of those churches which did survive. Another orgy of destruction took place under the Commonwealth, when episcopacy was abolished and many of the cathedrals were shut up, often after rough treatment by Cromwell's soldiers. At Peterborough Dean Patrick recorded how, in 1643, 'in a short time, a fair and godly structure was quite stript of all its ornamental Beauty and made a ruthful spectacle, a very Chaos of Desolation and Confusion, nothing scarce remaining but only bare walls, broken seats and shatter'd windows on every side.'

By the 18th century the gradual process of decay, neglect and botched repairs had reduced many cathedral churches to a sorry, and, in the case of Ely, perilous condition. Restoration gathered pace during the 19th century, often attracting much controversy, although the work of the likes of J L Pearson and Sir G G Scott was better informed than what had gone before. Only rarely, as in the case of the works by the amateur architect Lord Grimethorpe at St Albans, was it unredeemed by any hint of sensitivity.

Wymondham Abbey from the south-east. AFK

19

Binham Priory, Norfolk
12th–13th century

TF 982399. 4 miles (6.4 km) SE of
Wells-next-the-Sea, off B1388 Great
Walsingham–Blakeney road

[C] EH

Binham Priory was founded in about
1091 by Peter de Valoines as a daughter
house of St Albans. The east end was
demolished after the Dissolution leaving
the 12th-century nave, which was later
shorn of its aisles, as the parish church.
It still stands within a walled precinct
with a gatehouse, the craggy flint ruins
of the monastery sprawling to the south.
Its setting is as peaceful and remote as
any parish church in Norfolk, but it is
only a few miles from Little
Walsingham, one of the most important
pilgrimage places in England, and must
itself have received many influential
guests. This is significant, for Binham
appears to have been in the vanguard of
the Gothic style in the mid-13th
century.

The monk chronicler Matthew Paris
of St Albans stated that the 'frontem
ecclesie', or front of the church, at
Binham was constructed by Richard de
Parco, who was the prior between 1226
and 1244. Taken at face value this would
make Binham's west window the earliest
surviving example of bar tracery in
England. Bar tracery a technical
innovation essential to the development
of the Gothic style, first used in the
rebuilding of Reims Cathedral after
1210. It was popularised in England by
the rebuilding of Westminster Abbey by
Henry III after 1245, which has
traditionally been accredited with the
earliest bar tracery in the country.

At Binham, the west window was
originally divided into four lights with
one large and two smaller cusped circles
above. This design had been used in the
nave of Amiens Cathedral (1220–39) and
was high fashion indeed for the 1240s in
England, but repairs in 1990 revealed no
clear evidence for later insertion. Only
the large oculus in the window head
with its exquisite stiff leaf cusps is still
glazed, the lower parts having been,

Binham Priory, west front. RCHME

from the 17th century onwards,
progressively filled with red brick. The
original iron armature or 'ferramentum'
which supported the glass is preserved
inside the church.

Disguising the weighty Romanesque
nave beyond, the intricate facade is
highly decorative in a characteristically
English mode, with a subtle modulation
of the wall planes in light and shade. The
aisle fronts, now mere fragile screens,
frame the open sky.

20

Castle Acre Priory, Norfolk
12th–16th century

TF 814148. 3½ miles (5.6 km) N of
Swaffham on A1065

[A] EH

The Cluniac Order was introduced into
England at Lewes in Sussex by William
de Warenne, Earl of Surrey. He had been

granted the manor of Castle Acre after
the Conquest and built the castle. It was
his son William, the 2nd earl, who
founded the priory in about 1090.

The mother house of Cluny in
Burgundy was the epitome of monastic
magnificence and Castle Acre Priory
shared something of the same spirit of
architectural abundance. The west front
of *c.*1140–50, with its multiple tiers of
arcading, elaborately moulded arches
and decorated stringcourses now stands
in stark contrast with vast areas of
exposed rubble corework. Wherever the
ashlar facing does survive, it is richly
carved with a riot of decoration. There
are spiral piers like those of Durham and
Waltham Abbey (E), rope moulded
bases, scallop capitals, chevron and
billet moulded arches. At the crossing
and east end the massive piers are
banded in contrasting yellow and white
ashlar in Byzantine fashion.

The scale of the ruins of church and
monastic complex, which at its height
housed about thirty monks, are
impressive and convey an excellent
impression of the original layout. The
church followed the standard
Benedictine plan of an apsidal chancel,
later altered to a square east end, flanked
by aisles and transepts with apsidal
chapels, and a central tower. To the
south lies the cloister with the chapter
house, and the undercroft and stairs to
the 'dorter' or dormitory ranged along
its east side. Running at right angles
with a vaulted channel over the stream
is the well-preserved reredorter (lavatory
block). The south side was the frater, or
refectory, with its kitchen to the west.

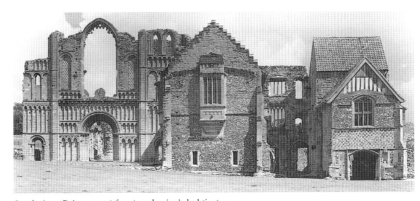

Castle Acre Priory, west front and prior's lodging. EH

Further out were the infirmary to the east, a later kitchen over the stream and some farm buildings beyond that to the south-west.

Best preserved is the part of the cloister adjoining the west front, which continued in residential use after the Dissolution. During the 14th century, the prior had adopted this range for his residence and a guest hall, with the accommodation on the first floor and a porch and storage below. As adapted in the 15th–16th century, the prior's chapel and study was a comfortable apartment with back-to-back fireplaces, a garderobe, smart oriel windows and a painted ceiling.

The Warenne Arms appear on the great flint and brick gatehouse which guards the entrance to the priory. The whole precinct, together with the village and its fine parish church of St James, was contained within the castle defences which were amongst the most extensive in England.

21
Ely Cathedral, Cambridgeshire
12th–19th century

TL 541801. Ely town centre
[C]

Of all the English medieval cathedrals, Ely has the most romantic silhouette. Its immensely long spine is punctuated by a soaring, solitary west tower and crowned by the spiky lantern of the Octagon. From a distance it dominates the flat fenlands for miles around. The simile of a great ship at sea is hackneyed, but would have been apt at the time of its building. Founded in 673 it was one of many monastic communities then springing up in the remote and misty fastness of the Fens. Largely cut off from the rest of the country by shallow water, the Isle of Ely was literally a law unto itself, over which the bishop (from 1109) ruled like a prince. Even before the great drainage works of the 17th century turned it into the most fertile farmland in England, the area was a rich source of revenue for the abbey, which kept vast flocks of sheep on the marshes.

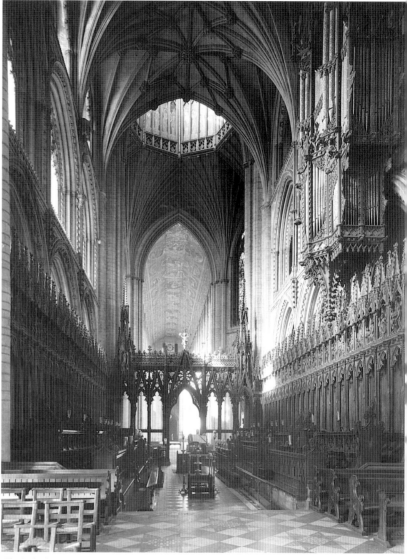

Ely Cathedral, choir and octagon, looking west. AFK

Financed by the abbey's wealth, the building of the cathedral church proceeded in a spirit of magnificence verging on megalomania, which culminated in the Octagon, one of the architectural wonders of the age.

The rebuilding of Ely Cathedral began in 1083 under Abbot Simeon and progressed westwards throughout the 12th century with an exaggeratedly long nave terminating in a massive west work. Both inside and out it is adorned with tier upon tier of arcading like a

gigantic wedding cake. The Romanesque building never reached absolute equilibrium – additions and rebuilding continued unabated into the 13th century. Bishop Northwold's east end, added between 1234 and 1252 to form a superior setting for St Etheldreda's shrine, is the apogee of pre-Westminster, lancet-style Gothic, out of date before it was finished. A hiatus followed until the beginning of the wondrous Decorated Lady Chapel in 1321, interrupted by the collapse of the central tower.

Genius is the only word to describe the man who conceived the idea of the Octagon. This expansion in all dimensions from the narrow constriction of the austere stone avenue of the nave is one of the most memorable of architectural experiences. Alan of Walsingham, the sacrist, was credited with it at the time. But it was the king's carpenter, William Hurley, who got the job of roofing this remarkable space, and this he achieved with the greatest panache, creating an illusionistic *tour de force* of a timber vault, posing with mad plausibility as stone.

By contrast, the rebuilt west bays of the choir are glorious but overblown and extravagant. Less indigestible are the grotto-like chantry chapels of Bishops Alcock and West of the late 15th and early 16th century, where Renaissance influence begins to creep in.

At the Dissolution the shrine had to go, but the Lady Chapel was kept as a parish church, after the decapitation of its figure sculptures. A good deal of the monastic buildings survive and are incorporated into the King's School, including the exquisite early 14th-century Prior Crauden's Chapel with its rare mosaic pavement.

In the 1640s the building was shut up altogether by Cromwell, who was Governor of the Isle of Ely (his house lies west of the cathedral). But where Cromwell's soldiers were thwarted, neglect and decay were equally potent destructive forces.

In the mid-18th century the architect James Essex carried out emergency repairs at a time when 'children were sent to play [in the cathedral] on wet days, coal carts were taken along the nave floor because traction was easier there than in the city streets, a Farriers forge occupied the baptistery and pigeons were bred and shot in the cathedral.' Although he altered the lantern, Essex averted collapse and Sir G G Scott was able to reconstruct the original form from his drawings 100 years later. The most visible Victorian contributions inside are the painted nave ceiling by Henry Styleman le Strange, Scott's lovely rood screen and the great crowned and finned iron

Gurney tortoise stoves which counter the Fens' piercing winds and foggy damp.

22

Norwich Cathedral, Norfolk
11th–19th century

TM 236088. On Tombland in town centre

[C]

The Romanesque cathedral church is exceptionally complete. The alterations necessitated by fate or fashion modified the original plan only slightly. Much the same is true of Peterborough (23, C), a building of similar size. But what sets Norwich apart is the fact that, like nowhere else in the region, its bishops achieved the vaulting in stone of the entire cathedral church from the later 15th century. The perfect synthesis between the two styles of architecture from either end of the medieval spectrum, with the great branching arcs of the vault rising in glorious contrast to the robust plasticity of the tall and narrow Romanesque nave, makes this the most successful and moving of interiors.

It was Bishop Herbert de Losinga (*d*.1119) who transplanted the cathedral from Thetford to Norwich in 1094, bringing with him the ancient throne of the East Anglian bishops. The Close dominates Tombland, the Saxon market place, and encompasses a huge area running down to the Water Gate at Pulls Ferry on the banks of the Wensum. It was to here that the Caen stone was transported from Normandy for the rebuilding of the cathedral. Many of the prosperous red brick and flint houses of the Close conceal the skeletons of monastic buildings. The Erpingham Gate, a superb showpiece of statuary erected *c*.1420 by the Agincourt veteran, Sir Thomas Erpingham, forms the main entrance to the outer court.

The west front (altered in the 15th century) is the least impressive aspect of the cathedral completed under Bishop Eboradus (1125–41), which is otherwise remarkable for its multi-tiered elevations, and wayward detailing of the

tower with its unmistakable 'portholes' and slender spire. Losinga's east end, of the grand apsidal type with radiating chapels as at St Edmundsbury Abbey (25, S), survives virtually intact in its lower parts, except for its east chapel. His idiosyncratic side chapels take an unusual two-storey form and a curious horseshoe shape with intersecting apses, aligned not quite due east. In the nave, the regular, insistent alternation of the stately piers is interrupted by two (formerly four) magnificent spiral-carved piers, like those found at Durham Cathedral and Waltham Abbey (E), which may have been designed to distinguish the nave sanctuary.

The fall of the spire during a storm in 1362 occasioned the rebuilding of the clerestory of the eastern arm with big windows in Perpendicular style. The transition from sombre nave to brilliant apse creates a compelling focus on the High Altar. And the apse, whose Romanesque arcades already had a remarkably strong vertical emphasis, rises transcendent to the wall-of-glass clerestory and Bishop Goldwell's web-like vault, of a century later.

Vaults, and a multitude of bosses, are also to be found in the exceptionally fine cloister, rebuilt, very slowly, after a fire in the late 13th century and not completed until about 1430. The Prior's Door, with its statuary applied metalwork-style to the arch, was probably designed by William Ramsey, one of a famous Norwich dynasty of masons which played an influential role in the development of the Perpendicular style.

23

Peterborough Cathedral, Cambridgeshire
12th–19th century

TL 194987. Peterborough town centre

[C]

Peterborough is a stately and consistent exercise in the mature Anglo-Norman Romanesque of the 12th century, topped and tailed by a piece of Perpendicular wizardry at the east end and an idiosyncratic early Gothic west front.

King Peada of Mercia founded the Benedictine monastery known as Medehamstede in the mid-7th century. The present name dates from the early 11th-century fortification of the monastery and part of the town. Traces of the Saxon church can be viewed under the south transept, and the Hedda stone, an important piece of Saxon sculpture dating from c.800, shaped like a shrine with a pitched roof with figures of the apostles beneath arcading, stands behind the High Altar. Hereward the Wake sacked the monastery in 1070, leaving it too impoverished for the Norman abbots to contemplate rebuilding until a fire of 1116 had destroyed the church. Much of the precinct survived the Dissolution, including the early 13th-century abbot's gate with its good figure sculpture. Henry VIII raised it to cathedral status in 1541. Two queens, Catherine of Aragon and Mary Queen of Scots, were interred here by Old Scarlett, the sexton, whose image presides over the nave.

The Romanesque work of 1118–95 takes its cue from Ely (21, C), but here the English love of decoration is becoming more pronounced. Inside, the subtle alternation of the shapes of the piers sets up a rippling rhythm, and a series of carved mouldings modulates and enlivens the heavy walls, in complete contrast to the weightiness of the nave of Ely. The aisles are lifted by their elegant early rib vaults and interlaced arcading. The overall effect is of an unusually unified and harmonious interior, tied together by the magnificent painted nave ceiling of the 1220s.

The insertion of traceried windows, sometimes into the old openings, could not disrupt the robust Romanesque skeleton, but rather forms a lacy membrane over it. Surprise and contrast are supplied by the steely filigree of fan vaulting of Abbot Kirkton's New Buildings, built by John Wastell beyond the apse in 1496–1508.

The medieval interior was subdivided by numerous screens and an incredible structure housing the High Altar 'of stone most exquisitely carved . . .

ascended by about a dozen steps . . . supporting a fair arched roof . . . [with] three goodly spires reaching almost to the top of the church.' But within two weeks in 1643 Cromwell's soldiers had reduced it to 'a very Chaos of Desolation and Confusion, nothing scarce remaining but only bare walls, broken seats and shatter'd windows on every side.' To J L Pearson is the credit due for reinstating it in the 1890s to its present serene splendour, with the marble pavements and a fine baldachino providing the new focus for the east end.

The architectural merit, or otherwise, of the west front, which had been completed after several changes of mind by 1238, has attracted much partisan comment. Critics have always been at odds. Horace Walpole commented that it was 'noble and in great taste' whilst A W N Pugin deplored it. It is essentially a screen facade of the type much loved by English medieval masons, which has been brought together with two other elements, triple giant niches and twin west towers at the ends of the aisles, to form a unique combination. Yet, as Francis Bond wrote, 'magnificent and poetic though it is, we have not the full effect

contemplated by the medieval builders'. The south-west tower was never built and a conventional porch was, ridiculously, inserted into the centre arch in the late 14th century. As originally intended, when viewed from the west, it would have built up into a crescendo of five spires, crowning the outer stair turrets, the twin towers, and the crossing tower beyond. This was a work of high drama. Unlike many screen facades which ignore the buildings behind them, at Peterborough the transition between external and internal space is particularly effective and the observer is compelled inwards by the great shadowed portals.

24

St Albans Cathedral, Hertfordshire
11th–19th century

TQ 145071. St Albans town centre [C]

'Of all our cathedrals none is so composite and heterogeneous as the ancient church of the Benedictine abbey

Norwich Cathedral choir, looking east. AFK

St Albans Cathedral, north arcade of nave, looking east. JB

of St Alban . . . a veritable architectural handbook, written in brick and stone.' So wrote Francis Bond of the great abbey church which was raised to cathedral status only in 1877. The earliest parts are amongst the best surviving examples of first generation Anglo-Norman work in the country. But enlargement and rebuilding continued apace fuelled by a combination of ambition, the demands of an important shrine and structural instability. The result is a church over 540 ft (164.5 m) in length in a glorious but uneasy confection of styles from the most austere Romanesque to full-blown Decorated.

The abbey owed its exceptional status (its head was made premier abbot of England in 1154) to the shrine of the earliest British martyr, the site of whose martyrdom had been marked by a church from as early as the 4th century. The enormous monastic precinct was almost totally destroyed after the Dissolution, but the nave continued to be used by the parish with the Lady Chapel as a grammar school. By the early 19th century neglect had left the west front a ruin and the rest in decay. Lord Grimethorpe took over the repairs after the death of Sir G G Scott, reputedly spending over £130,000 on his brash new west front and brutal external restoration. The interior, by contrast, retains more than most by way of original features including wall-paintings, shrine bases and great stone screens, which give some impression of the character of the medieval interior of a great abbey church.

The first Norman abbot, Paul of Caen, nephew to Archbishop Lanfranc, started the rebuilding on a massive scale in the 1070s. The transepts (remodelled by Grimethorpe) were completed within ten years and the nave by the dedication in 1115. This is an architecture of thick walls, whose monumental simplicity has an exaggerated austerity dictated by the use of reclaimed Roman brick, which was originally plastered and painted inside and out to resemble stone. The nave was extended in contrasting heavily moulded Early English style around 1200. In 1323 the Romanesque south arcade collapsed and was rebuilt in Decorated style

resulting in a disequilibrium which is restless and uncomfortable.

In the later 13th century Paul of Caen's magnificent east end was sacrificed to the cult of St Alban which demanded a much more spacious arrangement to accommodate the crowds of pilgrims and to display the shrine in a setting of suitable splendour. In about 1308 the reliquary was set on a fine new shrine base rising up in full view beyond the High Altar, lit by the huge geometrical traceried east window. Circulation was eased by a new retrochoir, giving onto the sumptuous Decorated Lady Chapel.

The shrine base was doubtless one of the first casualties at the Dissolution. The shattered fragments of Purbeck marble and clunch, still bearing traces of its painted decoration, were found and reassembled in 1872; a second complete restoration of the shrine was completed in 1992. Pilgrims were supervised from the carved wooden watching loft, clustered about by Perpendicular chantry chapels. The towering High Altar reredos of 1484 radically changed the emphasis of the choir, cutting off the shrine from view, suggesting that it was already by then waning in importance.

The wall-paintings preserved beneath many coats of limewash to be revealed and restored since the 19th century, convey an excellent idea of the original decorative scheme. A masonry pattern covered the walls, with figure paintings in significant positions. The nave piers are decorated with a remarkable sequence of 13th–14th century Crucifixions, scenes from the Life of the Virgin, and figures of saints which appear to have formed backdrops to altars set up against them.

25

St Edmundsbury Abbey, Suffolk
12th–20th century

TL 857643. Bury St Edmunds town centre

[A] EH

The destruction of the abbey church of St Edmund is the greatest loss of the

Dissolution of the Monasteries in East Anglia. The church, started by Abbot Baldwin (1065–97), was a gargantuan structure, over 500 ft (152.4 m) in length with a grand French-style eastern chevet raised up on a crypt, and a central crossing tower. The west front built by Abbot Anselm (1120–48) stretched to nearly 250 ft (76.2 m) in width, and was unmatched by any other English medieval church. Pierced by three giant recesses to the nave and aisles, it had at each end an apsidal chapel flanked by octagonal stair turrets, one of which remains. It was crowned by a lofty central tower added by Abbot Samson in the 1180s, which fell in 1430.

Rubble corework is all that remains of the ruins of the church, in the public gardens which occupy the site of the monastic precinct. The west front stands, a great hulk of flint masonry, denuded of its valuable stone facing, sunk into the present ground level by about 12 ft (3.6 m). Built into the three great arches are houses dating from the 18th and 19th century, and the labyrinthine interior (which is not open to the public) reveals the occasional springing of a vault or an angle shaft.

Founded in c. 663, the monastery was re-established by King Cnut in 1020. The relics of St Edmund, King of the East Angles who had been killed by the

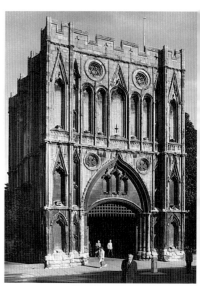

St Edmundsbury Abbey, the Great Gate. JB

Danes in 869, were translated to Baldwin's new church in 1095. After the Conquest, the veneration of Anglo-Saxon saints was, perhaps surprisingly, positively promoted and Bury, which also had the relics of St Botolph, gained particular status as the focus of an East Anglian royal cult. It accumulated vast estates, over which the abbot wielded total jurisdiction, and was the owner of the town, which Abbot Baldwin had laid out on its grid plan with a market whose revenues went to swell the abbey coffers.

The monastic precinct, enclosed by its walls running down to the banks of the River Lark, maintains a strong presence in the town with the mighty gatehouse facing the west front, erected by Anselm in the 1130s. A second gate which originally gave access to the outer court with its stables, service buildings and residential ranges, had to be rebuilt after the townspeople sacked and burnt the abbey in 1327. This so-called Great Gate combines the full repertoire of fanciful Decorated motifs, a crenellated silhouette with tiers of gabled ogee statue niches, bundles of vertical shafts like flagpoles and exotic star-patterned roundels with which it is embossed like a bejewelled box.

Two magnificent parish churches were built within the precinct. Adjoining the west front is St James, probably designed by John Wastell, restored by Sir G G Scott and enlarged by Stephen Dykes Bower after it became the cathedral early this century. St Mary's, begun c.1425, is one of the finest Perpendicular churches in the county.

To the south of the abbey church ruins lies the Great Churchyard with its jumble of mouldering tombs and headstones amidst the long grass. The most memorable inscriptions are now concentrated on the ruined 13th-century charnel chapel, including a stern warning to 'unguarded youth' against the 'allurements of vice and the treacherous snares of seduction'. It concerns a certain Sarah Lloyd, who 'suffered a Just but ignominious Death for admitting her abandoned seducer into the dwelling House of her Mistress in the Night of 3rd October 1799, and becoming the Instrument in his Hands of the crimes of Robbery and House-burning. These were her last words: "May my example be a warning to thousands".'

26

St Faith's Priory, Horsham St Faith, Norfolk
12th–16th century

TM 215152. Abbey Farm, 2 miles (3.2 km) N of Norwich off A140

[B]

The former Benedictine Priory of St Faith at Horsham, near Norwich, has the most impressive scheme of mid-13th-century wall-paintings in England. In quality they compare favourably with the best contemporary manuscript illumination. Like most English medieval wall-paintings, they are not true fresco, but the design was incised into dry plaster and painted in oils.

The paintings occupy what was once the east wall of the priory frater, or refectory, which was converted to a house after the Dissolution. A huge Crucifixion scene, the upper part of which had been destroyed, first came to light after a fire in the 1920s. This was a traditional subject for the refectory, where it was often combined with representations of the patron saint and major benefactors. Beneath it was found a strip of narrative scenes of the foundation legend (unique in England), relating how Robert and Sybil Fitzwalter were captured by brigands in the course of their pilgrimage in France. Only the miraculous intervention of St Faith saved them and in thanks they vowed to found a priory in her name on their return to England, which they did in 1105. On the far right of the strip is the ship bringing them safely home, and the final scene shows work in progress at the

St Faith's Priory, head of St Faith. EH

new priory, with the earliest known representation of a wheelbarrow.

Some retouching of the scenes was done around 1420 to update the costumes and architecture but no major alterations were made. The lower part of the walls had painted wall arcading, which was repainted at the same time with the brocade pattern often found on rood screens of the period.

Most striking of all is the larger than life-size figure of a crowned female saint, presumably St Faith herself, which flanks the Crucifixion. She had been covered by a wall built as early as the 14th century which preserved the freshness and immediacy of the painting, uncovered only in 1969. Her candid, uncompromising stare across a distance of seven centuries is thrilling, and mildly disconcerting. In style the figure resembles the contemporary illuminations of the celebrated Matthew Paris, monk of St Albans. The name of the master of the St Faith paintings is lost, but his work is of even greater beauty and sophistication.

4

Churches and Chapels

In East Anglia you are hardly ever out of sight of a medieval parish church. A few are pure architectural masterpieces, but most are a picturesque amalgam of varied styles and textures, imbued with a deep sense of history. Perhaps this explains the English fascination with them. The sheer quantity and variety are such that it is a daunting task to make a selection within the scope of this book. For the post-Reformation period the choice is much more restricted, but the region is remarkable for a number of idiosyncratic 'one-offs'.

Romano-British Christianity was extinguished by the settlement of eastern England by pagan Anglo-Saxons who were themselves eventually converted by the efforts of the ascetic Celtic church and missionaries dispatched from Rome. Nowhere illustrates this better than the simple and evocative 7th-century church of **St Peter on the Wall, Bradwell-on-Sea** (44, E), the best-preserved example of its date in the country.

Later Saxon churches are represented by the unique log-walled church of **St Andrew, Greensted** (33, E). Masonry structures of the period like the tower of **St John the Baptist, Barnack** (35, C) are characterised by long and short quoins and stripwork. Neither of these buildings is securely dated. Round towers are similarly difficult to date: most examples appear to have been built between the late 11th to mid-12th century, but they formed a strongly entrenched tradition which appears to have spanned the Conquest and continued as late as the 15th century. In Britain they are found almost exclusively in East Anglia (143 out of a total of 149), where they appear to attest to a longstanding cultural exchange with that part of northern Europe bordering the Baltic and North Sea where round towers are also found. The mid-12th century example at **St Margaret, Hales** (37, N), shows that Saxon building practices did not suddenly stop in 1066.

At the time of the Domesday survey of 1086, Suffolk already had 416 churches, around 75 per cent of its medieval total. The existing parish framework hardened into permanence at a time of massive rebuilding over the next century. A vital role was frequently played by the lord of the manor which explains the common proximity of churches to ancient manor house sites. At **St Michael, Copford** (42, E), the patronage of the Bishops of London produced an exceptional Romanesque rebuilding with a sophisticated scheme of wall-paintings. Hemel Hempstead (H) and Castor (C) have two of the finest 12th-century parish churches in the region.

So within a century of the Conquest most parish churches were already in existence. Some, like Hales, never grew any bigger. Total rebuilding was rare over the next couple of centuries, notable exceptions being the fine Early English **St Mary, West Walton** (41, N) and Felmersham (B). Most parishes could only afford to proceed by stages, lengthening the chancel, adding aisles, tower and porch and inserting larger, fashionable tracery windows into existing walls. Porches are one of the things that East Anglia does best, from the 14th-century carved timber north porch of Boxford (S) to the resplendent 15th-century two-storey stone version at **St Peter, Walpole St Peter** (43, N).

East Anglia is best known for its so-called wool churches of the 15th and early 16th centuries. Civic pride and personal piety led rich clothiers such as Thomas Spring of Lavenham (95, S) and John Clopton of Long Melford (S) to finance the rebuilding of their parish churches in grand style, and to found chantries for the welfare of their souls. They were able to employ master masons such as Reginald Ely and John Wastell, who created **King's College Chapel, Cambridge** (30, C). This project spawned a number of workshops which evolved a distinctive regional style,

St Mary, West Walton, church tower. Etching by John Sell Cotman, 1818. NMS

producing such masterpieces as Burwell (C) and Saffron Walden (E).

The character of the region's churches of all periods was dictated above all by the available materials. Before the Conquest timber was probably the norm. It proved an enduring tradition in Essex for towers like **St Laurence, Blackmore** (36, E) and Navestock (E). Barnack Quarry (C) supplied the stone for the cathedrals and its own parish church, but elsewhere the paucity of building stone meant that even the wealthiest parishes made sparing use of it. Most had to make do with flint and rubble covered with a coat of soft lime render to give the impression of stone. Flushwork is another East Anglian speciality, which made a virtue of the lack of stone by combining it in modest amounts to form elaborate patterns with knapped flint. Roman brick was sometimes re-used for dressings in rubble walls and the first English-made medieval brick, dating from the early 13th century, is found in this region. From the 15th century, brick was used extensively and to great decorative effect, especially for towers and porches.

The medieval interior on the eve of the Reformation was a riot of colour and carved woodwork. Timber roofs provided an opportunity for an extravagant display of gaudily painted carpentry and Suffolk is second to none in this respect: the amazing roof construction at the otherwise dull Needham Market has been likened to a second heavenly church hovering above the walls, triumphant hammerbeam roofs stagger with carving at Earl Stonham and flutter with angels at Woolpit. Only the West Country can rival the quality of East Anglia's woodwork fittings. The towering font canopy of Ufford (S), the painted screens of Bramfield (S) and Ranworth (N) and the carved benches of St Mary and St Germans, Wiggenhall (N) are supreme examples.

St George, Stowlangtoft (34, S) gives a good overall impression of the medieval interior as it survived the destruction of the Reformation, when such 'images as had been abused to superstition' had to be eradicated, along with the whole paraphernalia of

St Helen, Ranworth, panel from nave screen. AFK

medieval worship. The early 17th century saw much sober refitting with whitewashed walls painted with 'goodly sentences' and plain glass. **St Mary, Leighton Bromswold** (40, C) is an exceptional example of remodelling with a complete ensemble of fittings from this period. Many parish churches acquired new pulpits with the revival of preaching under James I, but the Commonwealth saw the removal of the recently installed communion rails,

fonts and such stained glass as may have survived. East Harling (N) and **Holy Trinity, Long Melford** (29, S) stored their glass, putting it back later.

New building was sparse during the 17th and 18th centuries, with little more than the rebuilding of a tower here and there. Euston (S) of 1676 and **All Saints, North Runcton** (27, N) of c.1700, rare rural examples of the influence of Wren's city churches, were exceptional. More extraordinary still was the Greek emple treatment given to **New St Lawrence Church, Ayot St Lawrence** (31, H) in the 1770s, a product of the Grand Tour and the first of its kind in England.

During the 19th century the absence of burgeoning industrial cities in the region meant that little new church building was needed to accommodate the masses. This is not the most fertile area for the study of Victorian architecture, and the best examples are exceptional rather than characteristic: the 'rogue' architect E B Lamb's **St Margaret, Leiston** (38, S) and the outlandish Booton (N), described by Lutyens as 'very naughty but built in the right spirit'. Holy Rood, Watford (H) is a sumptuous and original *tour de force* by the Catholic architect of Westminster Cathedral, J F Bentley. G G Scott, junior, and J O Scott's Roman Catholic St John Baptist, Norwich (N) of 1884–1910, was built to cathedral proportions in correct Early English style, curiously untouched by the new freedom of expression of the Arts and Crafts Movement. True Art Nouveau is rare in England, and the synthesis of architecture and fittings at **St Mary, Great Warley** (39, E) was exceptionally close in spirit to the Continental style. The concrete version of Suffolk Perpendicular by Mason and Erith at Felixstowe (S) of *c.*1930 and Lutyens' unfinished Italianate brick St Martin's, Knebworth (H) also demand a mention.

The 'High Church' ideals of the Ecclesiological Society are better represented in restoration than new building. The Ecclesiologists, influential proponents of a correct and hierarchical Gothic Revival style, advocated a return to a 'Catholic past', which involved stripping out 18th-century galleries and box-pews and reinstating the focus on the High Altar. By the beginning of the century many country churches had been reduced by centuries of neglect and piecemeal repairs to 'an exquisite state of decay', depicted by J S Cotman and Ladbrooke in their collections of engraved views. The wave of Victorian restoration and refitting reached its height in the years between 1860 and 1880. It is no coincidence that the end of this decade saw William Morris found

the Society for the Preservation of Ancient Buildings. The Society's protestations saved Blythburgh (S) from a thoroughgoing restoration, thus preserving its airy, pre-Victorian atmosphere.

Nonconformity has a long and impressive pedigree in the region. At first, Dissenters were forced to meet secretly in private houses. The earliest chapels were of necessity discreetly tucked away, discrete and often outwardly of domestic form. The Old Chapel at Walpole (S), built as a house in 1607, made a chapel in 1647 and enlarged after 1689, is one of the earliest in the country and has a wonderfully unspoilt interior. It was not until after the Act of Toleration of 1689 that Dissenters could build openly, which they soon began to do in some style. In Ipswich, the timber-framed **Unitarian Meeting House** (46, S) of *c.*1700 was the smart town cousin to Walpole and makes an interesting contrast to the fine red brick chapel in Bury St Edmunds (S) of 1712. Norwich has two exceptional chapels, the Old Meeting House of 1693 and the Octagon Chapel of 1756. At **Roxton** (32, B), a barn was converted to a chapel in a lighthearted Picturesque style much in vogue during the Regency.

27

All Saints, North Runcton, Norfolk
18th century

TF 646159. In North Runcton, 3 miles (4.8 km) SE of King's Lynn, off A10 (T) or A47 (T)

[C]

All Saints is a rare thing; an early 18th-century classical church built outside London. In 1701, North Runcton's medieval church collapsed in a gale, 'beaten down flatt to the ground by the fall of the steeple.' An appeal was launched and subscriptions were invited for the building of a new church. One of the trustees in charge of the rebuilding was Henry Bell, wealthy linseed oil merchant, ex-Grand Tourist, amateur architect and Mayor of King's Lynn.

All Saints, North Runcton. NC

These accomplishments (and a generous subscription of £15) made Bell the obvious choice as architect of the new All Saints.

In the 1670s and 1680s Bell had done good work in King's Lynn (94, N) and in Northampton, where he re-planned part of the town centre and built a grand classical-style church. All Saints, North Runcton is a smaller country cousin of All Saints, Northampton. It is built of local brick and brown carstone, much of it hidden beneath later cement render. The plan is simple; west tower, square nave, deep chancel. Inside, the nave has four Ionic columns with garlanded capitals of the type which Bell liked and used elsewhere, and a domed ceiling. The chancel has oak panelling, with Corinthian pilasters and entablature. In 1803 the organ chamber was added. Less sensitive was the later removal of the original pews and gallery. A fine 18th-century candelabra remains hanging in the nave.

Churches in the English classical style which blossomed after the Restoration are few and far between. Bell was an inventive architect and had plenty of ideas of his own, but All Saints undoubtedly owes something to Dutch influence and to Christopher Wren's rebuilding work after the Great Fire of London. The use of brick and stone, the oval and round-headed windows, the squared proportions and architectural treatment of the interior take their cue from the improvising moods and styles of Wren's fifty-one new London churches. All Saints is one of those sermon-tasting churches where the rich language of the Authorised Version was heard and Baptism, Marriage and Holy Communion took place according to the Book of Common Prayer.

28

De Grey Mausoleum, Flitton, Bedfordshire
17th–19th century

TL 059359. Inside church of St John the Baptist, Flitton, 2 miles (3.2 km) SE of Ampthill off A507

[B] EH

'Splendid in ashes, and pompous in the grave', here lie the de Greys of Wrest Park, in a mausoleum tacked on to the church of St John the Baptist. Wrought-iron gates lead into the de Grey 'gallery' of tomb-chests, effigies, epitaphs and paraphernalia of death. It is a good place to spot the changing fashions and styles of funerary sculpture, and what is lacking in first-rate quality is made up for in sheer vigour and earnestness. The earliest tombs are near the gates, the most recent further in.

Henry Grey (d. 1614) and his wife lie recumbent on a tomb-chest; spiky-crowned Jacobeans haunted by incredibly realistic skulls, and a lovely winged hourglass. More sophisticated is the monument erected to the next Henry Grey (dated 1658): marble effigies and a back wall boasting two Mannerist allegorical figures; one with a wantonly exposed breast.

Lady Jane Hart reclines beneath a robust inscription of 1673, her crumpled winding sheet a poignant contrast to the naive, up-and-down lettering. The baroque memorial to Elizabeth Talbot (d. 1681) is a suave architectural sculpture with veined Ionic columns,

De Grey Mausoleum, Flitton, detail of monument to Lady Jane Hart. RCHME

trailing fruits, and a scrolled pediment with a dog and a griffin supporting a lozenge.

In the north room are a pair of monuments to youthful Henrietta de Grey (d. 1716) and Henry de Grey (d. 1717); relaxed-looking figures on tomb-chests flanked by flaming urns, with obelisks behind. Close by is Anthony de Grey (d. 1723) life-size and alert in Roman dress; lying on a black-keeled sarcophagus. This was by the obscure John Dowyer who went in for uncomfortable poses and ghoulish effects – like the griffins' forked tongues and the sarcophagus's clawed feet.

The east room contains the finest monument, to yet another Henry de Grey and his two wives. Dated 1740, the figure of Henry is attributed to the great Rysbrack. Across the room is an austere neo-classical memorial to Philip, Earl of Hardwicke (d. 1790): bread-and-butter work by Thomas Banks who turned out dozens of similar busts and monuments. More fun is Baroness Grantham's (d. 1830) wall-tablet, with chocolate-box cherub, curly-edged cartouche and pantomime coronet.

The sentimental monument to Henrietta de Grey (d. 1848) is unmistakable Victorian hack-work: an angel bears the soul heavenwards above a tableau of busily grief-stricken figures. Nearby, Philip de Grey (d. 1859) snoozes away in white marble. This is a good place to stop, one's mind reeling with coats of arms, black and white marble and the celebration of death.

29

Holy Trinity, Long Melford, Suffolk
14th–20th century

OS 865467. Long Melford, 3 miles (4.8 km) N of Sudbury, at junction of A1092 and A134

[C]

Pevsner described Long Melford as 'one of the most moving parish churches of England, large, proud and noble'. It stands at the head of the green which expands from the long village street. On one side the fantastical turreted silhouette of Melford Hall peeps over a high wall, echoing the red brick of the Trinity Hospital, beyond which looms the great form of the church.

Long Melford was one of the prosperous cloth towns of the Essex–Suffolk borders and amongst the richest possessions of St Edmundsbury Abbey (25, S). The abbots had a house on the site of Melford Hall, which at the Dissolution passed to Sir William Cordell, builder of the present Hall and Hospital, who is commemorated by a fine Renaissance tomb in the church.

Flushwork and insistent Perpendicular tracery are the keynotes of the nave and chancel which form a single vessel with a cliff-like east end, beyond which projects the Lady Chapel. Rebuilding took place between c. 1460 and 1496. Towards the end of the period John Melford of Sudbury (S) was hired to complete it. He was a pupil of Reginald Ely, the influential first architect of King's College Chapel, Cambridge (30, C). The motif of tracery descending from the clerestory to form wall panelling, which the interior shares with several of the finest churches in East Anglia, is typical of his style. The four-square tower by G F Bodley skilfully encases a brick structure built after lightning destroyed the medieval tower in 1711.

Rebuilding was financed by 'the well disposed men of this town', wealthy clothier families whose names are recorded in flushwork inscriptions. The most important donors are depicted

Holy Trinity, Long Melford. AFK

kneeling in rich, heraldic costume in the stained glass, collected together into the north aisle windows, the finest in the county. Chief amongst them were the Cloptons of Kentwell Hall. John Clopton (d.1497) takes pride of place with his tomb, which doubled as an Easter Sepulchre, built into a recess between the sanctuary and the Clopton Chantry. This exquisite little chamber is a rare survival of the late-medieval fashion of employing a priest to sing masses for the soul of the founder, his family or friends. A tiny, fan-vaulted vestibule with its own fireplace leads into the chantry, the starry, painted scrollwork roof of which bears verses by the monk John Lydgate of Bury (d.1440).

John Clopton's will of 1496 left the sum of 100 marks for the 'garnishing of our Lady Chapel and the cloister there about'. This extraordinary building, almost like a separate church, has an inner sanctum encircled by its 'cloister' or wide ambulatory with a lovely carved roof, clearly by the same hand as the chantry. Originally it was almost freestanding, but the intervening space was later made into a dwelling for the chantry priests.

For comparison, visit Denston (S) about 12 miles (19.3 km) to the north-west, a lovely unspoilt village church also paid for by the Cloptons and their circle.

30
King's College Chapel, Cambridge, Cambridgeshire
15th–16th century

TL 447584. Cambridge town centre, off King's Parade

[C]

The building of King's College Chapel spanned the passing of an age. Three royal dynasties contributed to its creation, the final stage of which witnessed the transition to a style of architecture better fitted to a new, more secular era. It was the Lancastrian King Henry VI who founded the college in 1446. He intended his chapel to be one side of an impressive court and to be built 'in large form, clean and substantial, setting apart superfluity of too great curious works of entail [carving] and busy moulding'. But his intentions were thwarted by his own downfall and the turbulent years of the Wars of the Roses. The designs of the first master mason Reginald Ely saw a number of changes in the hands of his three successors, John Wolryche, Simon Clerk and John Wastell, all fellow East Anglians. The failure to build the rest of the complex left the chapel, to quote Francis Woodman's *Architectural History of King's College Chapel* (1986), 'stranded on a sea of grass like some enormous monument in a park.'

The building history is far too complicated to detail here. Suffice it to say that the Yorkist Richard III's attempt to complete it came to an end with his

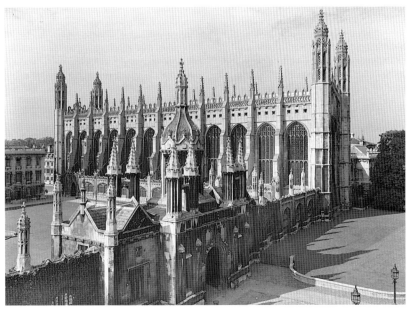

King's College Chapel, Cambridge, from the south-east. AFK

own defeat in 1485. It was not until 1508 that his successor Henry Tudor, preoccupied with his own projects at St George's, Windsor and his chapel at Westminster, could be persuaded to turn his attention to King's.

Comparison with the products of the Court workshop in the Fantastic style, represented in the region by the Alcock Chantry in Ely Cathedral (21, C), shows that the outcome of King's could have been very different, had it not been for the restraining hand of the last architect, John Wastell. As it was, the work far exceeded in elaboration the original intention, and Henry laid out a total of nearly £12,000, then a huge sum, to complete it. The insistent display of heraldry, in the form of superbly carved badges, is the mark of a king who felt the need to assert his claim after the incessant dynastic struggles of the preceding century. The crowning achievement of the interior, the stupendous high vault, was entirely Wastell's. It is indisputably, as Woodman wrote, 'the best planned, best-cut and best executed stone vault in England.'

Wastell's antechapel interior is the apogee of the Perpendicular style. Its transparency and steely linearity are fully in the tradition of Gothic royal chapels running back through St Stephen's Westminster to Ste Chapelle in Paris, both, in their way, seminal buildings for the development of that style. The transition to the Renaissance style is made by Henry VIII's screen and stalls which, though spectacular, are

heavy and earthbound in comparison with the great gilded cage in which they stand.

31

New St Lawrence Church, Ayot St Lawrence, Hertfordshire
18th century

TL 192169. 3 miles (4.8 km) W of junction 6, A1 (M) at Welwyn. Reached by a track through a field in Ayot St Lawrence

[C]

In the 1750s Englishmen became interested in archaeology. The Grand Tour began to take in wilder and remoter parts of Europe and Asia Minor. Books began to appear about the ruins of Palmyra, of Balbec, of Spalato and the Ionians. The 'Society of Dilettanti', a collection of rich young explorers, aesthetes and tourists led the way.

In 1751–5 the Society paid for two of its members, James Stuart and Nicholas Revett, to travel to Greece, a country still deliciously veiled in mystery. They went, and found lonely white temples, hard sunlight, romantic scenery, tumbled antique stones. After their return to England both men began to practise as neo-classical architects.

One of Revett's few works was the small church at Ayot St Lawrence. It was designed for a fashionable knight, Sir

Lionel Lyte, and it has a Greek temple front; a sensational thing for England in the 1770s. The church was designed to do three things: it replaced an old medieval church (which was left to become a picturesque ruin), it served as an eye-catching mausoleum to Lyte and his wife, and it showed the world how daring its client and architect were. Its white-stuccoed, impeccably Greek portico was copied from the Temple of Apollo at Delos, but that is as far as archaeological accuracy goes. The symmetrical screens of columns and end pavilions hark back to the favourite English scheme for a Palladian country house.

The interior is small and Roman rather than Greek with short tunnel-vaulted transepts, a short east end with a screen of two columns and an apsidal west end. Coffered ceilings hint at Roman baths and palaces. A shock comes with a walk round the back of the church. The exterior is bare brick, like an old warehouse. A Greek temple was intended to be seen 'in the round' but Revett's church only makes sense when seen from the front, or from Sir Lionel Lyte's house a couple of fields away. That gives the game away: the church is an exquisite sham.

32

Roxton Congregational Chapel, Bedfordshire
19th century

TL 152545. In Roxton, 7½ miles (12 km) NE of Bedford, on A428 (T)

[C]

Roxton Chapel is a barn conversion in a simple, pastoral corner of Bedfordshire. The barn belonged to Mr C J Metcalfe, owner of Roxton Park. It was opened for preaching on 31 May 1808. The people who used it were Congregationalists who had split from a larger church at St Neots.

Congregationalists did not intend their buildings to look like 'proper' churches. Their new chapel was given the appearance of a cottage *orné* with deep thatched roof, tree-trunk colonnade, white rendered walls and

New St Lawrence, Ayot St Lawrence, the east front. RCHME

Roxton Congregational Chapel. RCHME

ogee-arched doors and windows. Two wings were added later in the same style, one containing the Sunday school the other the village school. Up on the roof three Oriental-looking ventilators recalled the Chinese Dairy at Woburn Abbey (B). Metcalfe was a man of taste and the chapel was meant as an ornament to his estate as well as a place with a serious use.

The interior is as plain and homely as a farmhouse kitchen: cream-washed walls, scrubbed brick floors; solid-looking benches and box-pews behind wooden screens. At the front, a pulpit and an organ. At the back a delightfully wonky gallery with creaking boards, narrow seating and the ceiling close overhead. Most of the glass in the leaded windows is clear, and the school rooms are suitably austere. A single exotic moment comes with the twig-work porch on the south wing, where a hidden door leads into a tiny panelled room furnished with table and chair. In this cramped place a Congregational minister might pray and prepare his fervent sermons. A small window looks out onto the chapel yard laid out like a private garden with grass, roses, shrubs and bent hawthorns. There are no burials here. Beyond the yard lies a slice of bright green parkland, with another cottage *orné* lodge perched on the horizon and away to the left, through the trees, the plum-coloured house where Metcalfe lived.

Despite its sweet and naive appearance things happened in this Nonconformist chapel. In 1839 the Church Book records that the 'divine presence and power were experienced by

many'. Artisans, labourers, poor people and free-thinking gentry came here, wrestled with the devil and met with God, while sheep grazed outside beneath the oaks of Roxton Park.

33

St Andrew, Greensted, Essex
?10th–19th century

TL 539030. 1 mile (1.6 km) SW of Chipping Ongar off A113. Also signposted from A414

[C]

Timber churches are mentioned by writers from 8th-century Bede to William of Malmesbury in the early 12th century and church excavations occasionally reveal traces of them. Before the Conquest timber churches probably outnumbered masonry structures in most areas, but were generally replaced during the period of intensive rebuilding in the century or so thereafter. Greensted is the sole surviving example of a log-walled church. The key to its survival may be that it was held in special veneration for an association with St Edmund (martyred 870), whose remains may have rested here on their journey back to St Edmundsbury Abbey (25, S) from London in 1013.

The nave walls are formed of upright logs from small oaks of less than a century's growth, split in half and reared with the curved face outside. The edges have been squared off and are grooved to hold thin fillets which help to keep the weather out. Each of the logs is bevelled into the wall-plate beneath the eaves. The corner posts, only one of which is original, are neatly contrived from three-quarter logs. The timber chancel was replaced in rust-red Tudor brick, extended and altered in the 18th and 19th centuries.

The present appearance of the church dates from Rector P W Ray's restoration of 1849 which he recorded in his *History of Greensted Church*. His restoration work included the reconstruction of the nave walls, using most of the surviving timber, but replacing the wall-plates, sills and plinths. The posts may originally have been sunk directly into the ground and could have decayed and been cut down several times before, which would account for the fact that the roof, which was said to have been 'heavy and without any particular character . . . consisted of a tie beam at less than six feet from the ground'.

Inside, the flat faces of the logs (now revealed) had at some time been plastered and perhaps painted. Despite restoration, it is not hard to envisage the

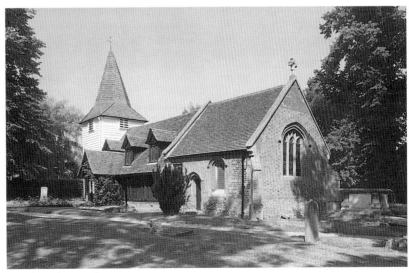

St Andrew, Greensted. AFK

flickering torchlit interior of the original thatched and windowless church.

Evidence of comparable log-walled structures has been found during excavations in southern Scandinavia; for example at Lund in Denmark where the church was founded by Cnut, ruler of England 1016–35. But this may well represent the final phase of a very long-lived tradition and it is currently impossible to date Greensted. Dendrochronology holds out the best hope of solving this particular mystery.

34
St George, Stowlangtoft, Suffolk
c.1400

TL 958682. 2 miles (3.2 km) SE of Ixworth off A1088

[C]

Stowlangtoft is one of the less well-known Suffolk churches. It deserves greater recognition for its fine collection of fittings. The building is an unusually unified composition in an austere Perpendicular style, having been built all at one time shortly before 1400. Robert Ashfield, the patron, lies buried in the chancel. The interior bears the scars of the inescapable strictures of the 16th-century Reformers. But the Revd Samuel Rickards, rector from 1832–64 and a keen supporter of the Oxford Movement, ensured a careful restoration under the direction of the architect William White. He also installed the gaily decorated organ, purchased at the Great Exhibition of 1851.

There are many clues to the medieval interior. On the north wall, placed, as usual, opposite the main door where it would confer protection on those entering the church, is a huge painted St Christopher. An iron-bound door and chest betray the original use of the tower as a strongroom. The font with its mutilated figures of saints is contemporary. But what sets the church apart is its woodwork. The nave has rank upon rank of later 15th-century benches with carved backs, ends and buttressed armrests bearing grotesques. Unlike

St George Stowlangtoft, nave benches. ES

Blythburgh's series of the Vices and Labours of the Months, no particular themes emerge here. Some of the more exotic specimens from the bestiary are represented, including the mermaid (with her evil reputation of luring men to destruction), a harp-playing boar, cockatrice, camel and unicorn, plus Scandal in the form of a writer with inkwell. A few excellent 19th-century copies by Henry Ringham of Ipswich complete the set.

The magnificent chancel stalls are amongst the finest in England; all of a piece with the screen which bears the arms of Robert Ashfield, they are contemporary with the church. Misericords carved with symbols of the Evangelists are flanked by armrests with exotic bearded heads. The finials are peopled by a whole cast of a service: a pair of priests in pulpit and prayer desk, two taperers, cantors bearing the arms of Ashfield and Peche and the servers with incense boat and Gospel book.

The great Rood, or Crucifix, had to be dismantled at the Reformation and the rood loft went with it. But Stowlangtoft retained its painted canopy of honour bearing the sacred monogram IHS which is paralleled at Metfield (S). Painted bosses on the chancel roof are all that remains of a similar canopy to

the High Altar. To complete the inventory of fine woodwork there is an imported set of superb Flemish Renaissance carvings of the Passion.

35
St John the Baptist, Barnack, Cambridgeshire
Pre-Conquest–15th century

TF 079051. 3 miles (4.8 km) SE of Stamford, off B1443

[C]

Barnack was famed for its fine oolitic limestone, which was quarried to the west of the village (in the area now called the Hills and Holes). Already in use in the Roman period, the quarry became finally worked out by the 15th century, having supplied stone for the abbey churches of Norwich (22, N), Ely (21, C), Peterborough (23, C), and many others. The most important village in the Soke of Peterborough, Barnack was owned by the abbey throughout the Middle Ages.

The church of St John is a richly sculptural building which makes a splendid showcase for its native stone. It is a fine grained ashlar, weathered to a cool silver, whose qualities invite

St John the Baptist, Barnack, the tower. JC

carving and sculptural invention. Every part of the church from the pre-Conquest tower, to the late 15th-century Lady Chapel, demonstrates a passionate love of decoration allied to a feeling for grand sculptural effects.

The tower which was built probably in the late 10th–early 11th century, is constructed of rubble stone which would originally have been rendered, articulated by ashlar long and short quoins and plain, flat mouldings. It is a massive elemental structure, decorated with applied features in an unarchitectural fashion. Vertical strips of stone, framed by horizontal bands, divide the surface into segments. Windows, doors and richly carved scrollwork plaques are scattered on the surface, some within the segments, others cutting through the pilasters, seemingly at random, encrusting the tower like jewels on a reliquary. The stumpy early 13th-century spire is one of the earliest in England.

The rest of the building comes as an unexpected bonus. The transitional (i.e., late 12th-century) nave arcades still have round arches, adorned with chevron moulding to the earlier, north side. In the 14th century the aisles were remodelled with elegant curvilinear windows. The 13th-century porch, an early vaulted example, was left untouched, its massive construction in vibrant contrast with the finely moulded arch and ranked colonnettes inside with wiry stiff-leaf capitals. Ballflower decoration, typical of the 14th century, appears on the east window with its extraordinary crocketed gables in the tracery, like the east window of the Lady Chapel at St Albans Cathedral (24, H). Barnack's own Lady Chapel (otherwise known as the Walcot Chapel), at the east end of the south aisle, was built c.1500. It has severe Perpendicular windows, but a quatrefoil plinth and an unbridled outbreak of tracery decoration to the crenellated parapet.

Further sculptural joys are to be found inside, chief amongst which are an iconic Romanesque effigy of Christ, discovered buried beneath the floor in 1931, and an early 13th-century font. Not to be outdone, the churchyard contains one of the most extraordinary

monuments to be found anywhere, in the form of a recumbent palm tree commemorating a certain George Ayscough Booth, 'gentleman cadet of Sandhurst', who died in 1866.

36
St Laurence, Blackmore, Essex
12th–16th century

TL 603016. 4 miles (6.4 km) E of Chipping Ongar off A414

[C]

Round towers are East Anglia's speciality, but Essex, individual as ever, has its own particular theme: the timber tower. Blackmore's is one of the most impressive, belonging to a distinctive type which it shares with Margaretting (E) and Bulphan (E), described as a group by Cecil Hewett as 'the ultimate development of medieval belfries in this county'. Navestock (E) is the earliest, probably late 12th–early 13th century, and is also worth seeing.

Timber remained the dominant building material in Essex for domestic buildings well beyond the Middle Ages. Long after the demise of complete wooden churches like St Andrew, Greensted (33, E), timber continued to be used in churches for towers, bell turrets and porches and is occasionally found in more unexpected places, like the nave arcades at Shenfield (E).

Strictly speaking Blackmore does not belong in this section, as it was the church of a small Augustinian priory. But as a group the towers belong to parish churches, and there are no monastic remains here. Even the choir has gone, leaving only the nave which was always in parochial use.

The late 15th-century tower, abutting a Romanesque west wall, adopts the usual pagoda-like silhouette of diminishing stages, clad in weatherboarding beneath a shingled spire. Unusually complete, the tower retains delicate traceried windows and part of the framing is now shown off on the outside. Inside, the experience is of a forest of honey coloured oak,

St Laurence, Blackmore, interior of tower.
P ROGERS/ECC

bewildering at first in its complexity. Its massive construction, buttressed by aisles and stiffened with curving cross bracing, was needed to withstand the stresses and strains of the tolling of weighty bells.

37
St Margaret, Hales, Norfolk
12th century

TM 384961. 5½ miles (8.8 km) NW of Beccles, E of A146

[A]

The round tower and the thatched roof are just as much a part of the Norfolk scene as the soaring Perpendicular tower in the wide open landscape. Round church towers in Britain are almost exclusively found in East Anglia, 143 still standing at the last count, of which 125 are in Norfolk. Most are in the south-eastern quarter of the county, between Norwich and the coast. Thatch must once have been the commonest roof covering for the more humble, rural parish churches. A survey in 1831 recorded as many as 270 in the county, although less than a quarter of those survive today.

St Margaret, Hales. JC

St Margaret's is an unusually well-preserved small Romanesque parish church, dating to the second quarter of the 12th century. The unaisled nave and apsidal chancel have survived intact only heightened to allow for the insertion of taller windows in the late 13th–early 14th century. The tower, although cruder in its detailing, can be seen to have been added to the nave shortly after completion. Inside its base is a pair of blocked double-splayed round windows still bearing the imprint of the basket work centring which was used to construct them, a rare survival of Saxon technique.

The walls display a wonderfully mellow patina of neatly coursed flint and rubble peeping through an eroded covering of soft lime render, contrasting with the fine grained ashlar dressings. The masons revelled in the luxury of the stone, cutting roll mouldings, neat nookshafts and cubic capitals, with arcading around the apse. The north and south doors are a riot of crisply carved invention in three orders with wheels, chevrons and bobbins.

The interior has a simple dignity. The sober whitewashed scheme of the 18th century with its pulpit and west gallery found room for a 15th-century font and the traceried dado of the rood screen,

and has been softened by the recent uncovering of parts of the medieval wall-paintings. A great St Christopher stands opposite the north door, with St James in the south-east window reveal and a pair of angels flanking the chancel arch.

Like many Norfolk churches, St Margaret's stands in isolation amongst fields, ½ mile (0.8 km) from the ancient common at Hales Green (the site of the Hobart family's Hall with its magnificent barn) and over ½ mile (0.8 km) away from Hales village. One of the ever-increasing numbers of Norfolk churches no longer in use for worship, St Margaret's has been placed in the care of the Redundant Churches Fund.

38

St Margaret, Leiston, Suffolk
1853–4

TM 438624. Leiston. 3¼ miles (5.2 km) NW of Aldeburgh on B1122. Church to W of town centre of B1119 Saxmundham road

[C]

Garrets engineering works brought prosperity to mid-19th-century Leiston. The old church was no longer able to accommodate the growing population

and the decision was taken to demolish it, keeping the medieval tower, and to build a new church 'suited to this district – plain, neat and characteristic, and to accommodate 840 parishioners.' An account in *The Builder* for the year 1854 tells a familiar tale of a thatched church in decay after centuries of neglect and botched repairs, so that 'the building was left merely a huge plastered tube, ugly, inconvenient, and rotten . . . The east wall had been rebuilt in red brickwork; the window was circular headed, with a wooden *three-bay solid frame*.'

The impropriety of all this was offensive to Victorian sensibilities and the strictures of the Ecclesiologists, High Church promoters of a strict vision of church building and fitting out in accordance with a medieval, Catholic, past. But here the parish was under the influence of an Evangelical rector, the Revd John Calvert Blathwayt, who wanted a spacious preaching auditorium, so the result was not to be an Ecclesiologist set piece. With the patronage of the Hon. Miss Thellusson of Leiston Abbey and a small grant from the Incorporated Church Building Society, the architect, Edward Buckton Lamb, was employed in 1853–4 to build the new church at a cost of £2,500.

Most of Lamb's work was commissioned by Evangelical or Broad church incumbents and he favoured the spacious centralised plan, like an adapted 'preaching box', with low walls and a complex roof structure. True to form, *The Ecclesiologist Journal* described St Margaret's as 'a noticeable exhibition of all those eccentricities which render Mr Lamb the most affected and *outré* . . . of all our ecclesiastical architects.'

To the medieval tower Lamb added a building of Greek cross form with an elongated west arm and an entrance porch to the north. The walls are of flint banded with hammer-dressed Kentish ragstone and dressings in a finer Caen stone. The exterior displays a profound feeling for texture and soft muted colours, although the original roof of

St Margaret, Leiston, looking east. AFK

St Mary, Great Warley, looking north-east. JB

grey tiles with a diaper pattern of picked-out fishscale tiles has since been replaced. The many-gabled silhouette with a spirelet and the quirky detailing is typical of Lamb's persistently eccentric and Picturesque vision, which has earned him the title of Arch Rogue amongst Victorian architects.

The flamboyant roofs dominate the interior, overgrown hammerbeams in the nave with huge traceried spandrels and a fantastic corona over the crossing, in the true spirit of the Decorated style, with its aptitude for clever spatial effects.

The Grand Reopening of the church took place on 31 August 1854. The occasion was marked by the closure of Garrets for the day, with a dinner of roast beef and plum pudding laid on for the poor, aged and children, followed by tea and amusements at the Old Abbey.

39
St Mary, Great Warley, Essex
1902–4

TQ 589900. To S side of B186, near junction 29, M25, ½ mile (0.8 km) S of Great Warley

[C]

The church of St Mary, Great Warley, is like an architectural geode, the roughness of the exterior leaving one totally unprepared for the exquisite richness within. Designed in 1902–4 by Charles Harrison Townsend with fittings by William Stephens Reynolds, this is a virtuoso Arts and Crafts version of Art Nouveau, as close in spirit to the Continental style as anything in England.

The roughcast Voyseyesque exterior with its battered buttresses, yellow sandstone dressings and sweeping tiled roofs, represents a beau ideal of an early medieval church, with its unaisled nave, transepts, raised chancel and apse. Inside, the senses are assailed by a panoply of gorgeous materials, mellow woods, coloured marbles, metals, enamels, glass and mother of pearl, combined with fertile invention into organic forms. Broad bands of plaster reliefs finished in aluminium leaf clasp the timber vault and glimmer in the light of the iron electroliers, from which pendant light bulbs emerge like exotic fruits or buds. A pair of great-winged angels enfold the font. Sinuous trees support the arms of the beaten metal cross of the pulpit front. Entwining wild rose trees compose the rood screen with mother of pearl petals and big red rosehips, or pomegranates, like wrapped toffee apples.

But this is no mere decoration for decoration's sake, for architecture and fittings are fused together into an intense synthesis, redolent with symbolism. Rich and dark, the barrel vaulted nave forms a tunnel, emerging into the transcendent apse. Its gleaming walls, embossed with the sacred vine with crimson fruits like drops of blood, are enclosed by the spiky crown of thorns altar rail. At its heart, the focal point for the whole church, the reredos with its shining, triumphant figure of Christ, standing upon the cornelian-eyed serpent.

40

St Mary, Leighton Bromswold, Cambridgeshire
13th–17th century

TL 115753. 4½ miles (7.2 km) W of Huntingdon, off A604

[C]

Church building was generally at a low ebb at the beginning of the 17th century, depressed by the aftermath of the Reformation. But at St Mary's something of a religious revival was in the offing, at the hands of the orator and metaphysical poet George Herbert, ordained deacon in 1626, and his friend Nicholas Ferrar, who founded the ascetic religious community at the neighbouring Little Gidding (C). Under the patronage of the Duke of Lennox, the ruinous 13th-century parish church was given a major facelift by relinquishing the aisles to form an unencumbered preaching box with new roofs, a fine tower and remarkable set of fittings.

The tower is the first thing to meet the eye, a chaste and dignified exercise

in the finest-jointed ashlar, displaying a curious classical clothing of Gothic form, topped by obelisks with ball finials. The story of the medieval development of the church can be read in window tracery, while the extraordinary rainwater heads supply a date of 1632 for the rest.

Herbert brought Leighton Bromswold to the forefront of the religious culture of the day. Preaching, having suffered a setback immediately after the Reformation, was now back in vogue and a flood of new pulpits followed James I's edict that every church should have one. Double and

triple deckers began to appear, but Herbert went one better and installed an almost identical pair of pulpits, one of which functioned as the reader's desk, to ensure that the service and sermon were given equal weight.

Matching stalls and benches focus on the central space, with a low screen to the chancel and a communion rail across the east end. It was only after the Reformation, when the congregation gained access to the chancel for the first time and rood screens were often done away with altogether, that these rails became necessary. In 1636, in accordance with the reforms of

St Mary, Leighton Bromswold. ES

Archbishop Laud, Bishop Wren of Norwich (97, N) ordered that 'the Rayle be made before the communion Table reaching crosse from the North wall to the South wall, neere one yarde in height, so thick with pillars that doggs may not get in.'

41

St Mary, West Walton, Norfolk
13th century

TF 471133. 1½ miles (2.4 km) N of Wisbech off B198

[C]

Cotman's etching of 1813 depicts the detached tower of West Walton church exactly as it appears today, the massive structure straddling the churchyard entrance like a gatehouse. The tower rises up in four stages, clamped together by the great polygonal buttresses, their original caps replaced by a later parapet and pinnacles which look fiddly and out of scale by comparison. It is a superbly sculptural piece, its multiple-recessed planes unified by an overlay of tiers of arcading.

When Cotman set out to draw 'all the ornamented antiquities of Norfolk', most country churches were, as John Piper wrote, 'at an extreme of beauty. Ready to drop like over ripe fruit, they were in a state of exquisite decay.' The 1820s series of *Views of the Churches of Norfolk* by Ladbrooke depict a similar story of picturesque ruin, prior to the great wave of restoration which peaked in the 1860s and 1870s.

St Mary, West Walton is remarkably free of Victorian restoration and retains a strong sense of a medieval church whose development was stopped in its tracks, and was thereafter left unchanged and slowly mouldering for centuries. Constructed in Barnack stone, it is an unusually sumptuous example of parish church architecture of the mid-13th century. The manor belonged to the wealthy Castle Acre Priory (20, N), one of whose priors is commemorated by a fine bearded effigy in St Mary's north aisle.

St Mary, West Walton. JC

The tower's polygonal buttresses are echoed on the south porch and the west front, where they have been covered by the enormous raking buttresses propping the wall. Arcading, colonnettes, intricate mouldings with dogtooth and windswept stiff-leaf capitals, leitmotifs of the Early English style, are masterfully handled. The truncated arcading inside the porch and on the clerestory reveals that the aisles have been enlarged. The north and south doors, as frequently happened, were re-set, being considered too good to discard. Lancet windows, which were the order of the day, have been superseded in the south aisle by tracery. At the east end is a very fine fully fledged geometrical window of the later 13th century. The chancel has lost its aisles and the east wall was rebuilt in 1807.

Inside, the 13th-century splendour of the arcades contrasts with the wide, spartan aisles. Piers ringed with rich Purbeck marble shafts and vigorous stiff-leaf capitals call upon Ely (21, C) and Lincoln cathedrals for inspiration. Wall-paintings of various dates mingle on the upper walls. The steep 13th-century roof has given way to a lavish 15th-century construction of alternating tie beams and hammerbeams, adorned with angels. Like St Peter, Walpole St Peter (43, N), St Mary has its own locally made brass eagle lectern. In the south

aisle a painted board forms a poignant record of three great 17th-century floods.

42

St Michael, Copford, Essex
Early to mid-12th century

TL 935227. Copford Green, 6 miles (9.6 km) SW of Colchester off A12

(T)

[C]

St Michael, once known as 'Our Lady at Copforde', is a highly unusual church dating from about the second quarter of the 12th century, containing an unparalleled contemporary scheme of wall-paintings. Exceptionally for an English Romanesque parish church, it was originally vaulted, although the inexperience of the masons meant that the vault fell within a few centuries of construction. Its rare qualities may be explained by the patronage of the Bishop of London, who was lord of the manor, and whose chapel it may originally have been.

The tall nave has an apsidal chancel and unusually large shafted windows placed high in the walls. Wide pilaster buttresses reinforced in Roman brick were designed to support the vault. Towards the end of the 12th century the building was enlarged by cutting an arch through the south chancel wall to form a transept, and this was later extended westwards as an aisle under a sweeping catslide roof.

Marred by heavy restoration and unsightly pointing, the exterior is rather disappointing. Not so the interior, although the paintings were partly repainted and embellished by Daniel Bell on discovery in 1872, and waxed in the 1930s. The nave walls are adorned with an elaborate painted architectural framework into which narrative scenes and symbolic armed figures are set. Biblical scenes ran up into the vault, the only complete scene now being the

miracle of The Healing of Jairus's Daughter on the north wall above the pulpit. Bands of geometrical patterns converge upon the focal point of the Christ in Glory in the apse vault, the main outlines alone of which had survived under limewash, forming the basis for Bell's repainting.

Compared with typical provincial wall-paintings, St Michael was unusually complex and sophisticated in subject matter, style and technique. The closest surviving parallel is St Gabriel's Chapel in Canterbury Cathedral, but it may well have reflected contemporary painting at the long-vanished Romanesque St Paul's Cathedral, London.

43

St Peter, Walpole St Peter, Norfolk
c.1350–1435

TF 502169. 2 miles (3.2 km) N of Walpole Highway, off A47 (T)
[C]

The medieval wealth of the marshlands to the west of King's Lynn (94, N), between The Wash and the Fens, is attested to by a group of magnificent churches. From the Norman Walsoken (N) to the four Wiggenhalls (N) with their superb carved benches, they are all worth a visit. The so-called cathedrals of the marshlands, Terrington St Clements (N) and St Peter, Walpole St Peter, were recalled by Dorothy Sayers in *The Nine Taylors* (1934), which keenly evokes the inhospitable landscape in which they stand.

St Peter is a graceful Perpendicular structure dating from *c.*1350–1435. The sober and elegant tower, the earliest part, is dwarfed by the grand body of the church. The nave has considerable gravitas, although it is highly ornate in its upper parts. Broad aisle windows almost fill each bay with a sheet of glass, clamped together by a gridiron of tracery. Beneath the east end of the long chancel runs a low vaulted processional passage with massive carved bosses.

The finest bosses were reserved for inside the splendid stone south porch, dated by its prominently displayed heraldic devices as pre-1435. The large bosses of the branching tierceron vault depict the Assumption of the Virgin, the Last Judgment, and the Pietà, a rare subject in England. A veritable bestiary of dragon and hound, donkey and eagle keeps them company. A Notice requests all persons to remove their pattens before entering, and beside it hangs a pair of the same.

Inside, the horizontal emphasis of the exterior is transformed into glorious, soaring verticality by the tall and narrow nave crowned by a roof with alternating arch braces and tie beams. Yet the overwhelming impression is of open space, lit by raking shafts of

St Michael, Copford. P ROGERS/ECC

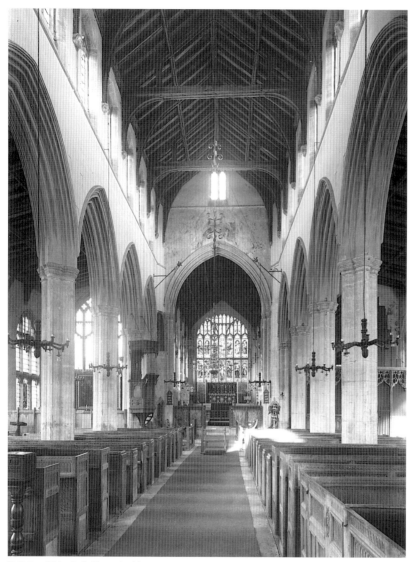

St Peter, Walpole St Peter, looking east. AFK

44

St Peter on the Wall, Bradwell-on-Sea, Essex
7th century

TM 031082. Bradwell-on-Sea.
Signposted from B1021. Chapel on
footpath from car park on Roman
road

[A]

St Peter's is a simple stone box standing
in a bleakly beautiful spot beside the
North Sea. Now seemingly deeply
remote, Bradwell was once of great
strategic importance as a safe landing on
this otherwise treacherous, marshy
coastline. The Romans erected there the
fort of Othona, like Burgh Castle (1, N),
part of the Saxon shore defences. The
Saxons adopted these convenient
strongholds for their own use and
eventually most of them came to house
important monastic sites.

The East Saxons who had colonised
the area after the Romans' departure,
proud of their pagan ancestry, had
thrown off the mantle of Christianity
extended to them by Bishop Mellitus,
sent from Rome with Augustine in
AD 597. But in AD 653 their king,

St Peter on the Wall, Bradwell-on-Sea. JB

sunlight from the huge windows. The
chancel, paid for by the Rochford family,
constables of Wisbech Castle (C), is
extraordinarily lavish for a parish
church, lined with canopied stone seats
for the chantry priests with nodding
ogee niches between the windows.

A wonderful collection of fittings
spans either side of the Reformation,
with medieval and Jacobean standing
cheek by jowl. In the nave, 15th- and
17th-century benches jostle 18th-
century box-pews. A Seven Sacrament

font of 1532 carries a towering Jacobean
cover. The pulpit with its tester is dated
1620, the brass eagle lectern is early
16th century, of East Anglian
manufacture, from King's Lynn or
Norwich. The painted saints of the rood
screen bear the scars of the Reformation.
A grand pedimented 17th-century screen
spans the entire width of the church
between the doors, to counteract
draughts. At the back of the church
stands an 18th-century parson's shelter,
like a sedan chair, for rainy funerals.

St Peter and St Paul, Salle, from the north-west. JB

Sigeberht, received the faith from his overlord, Oswy of Northumberland, who sent Cedd of Lindisfarne to be their bishop. Bede recorded how the saintly bishop 'built churches in several places, ordaining priests and deacons to assist him in the work of the faith, and the ministery of baptising, especially in the city which in the language of the Saxons, is called Ythancestir . . .' This was almost certainly Bradwell, which became for a very brief period the first cathedral in Essex.

The church was built in, or rather straddling the west wall of, the Roman fort, a short fragment of which survives in a thicket to the south. The Kentish ragstone, honeycombed volcanic tufa, septaria and Roman brick from which it is built were taken from the Roman walls. Originally it had an eastern apse separated from the nave by a pair of arches turned in Roman brick, the remains of which can be seen on the east wall. To each side was a rectangular chamber known as a *porticus*, a feature of Saxon churches.

The monastery was destroyed during the Danish invasions of the 9th century but the church was still being used as a chapel of ease to the parish church of St Thomas as late as the 16th century. It then became a barn, with large wagon doors piercing the side walls. Re-

consecration took place in 1920 after extensive repairs.

St Peter on the Wall's similarity to the Kentish group of early Saxon churches has led to some recent speculation that it may have been built only after the death of Cedd, when Archbishop Theodore reunited the diocese with London in 669, thereby returning it to the influence of Rome rather than the Celtic Church. Be that as it may, this remains by far the earliest identifiable church in the region and an evocative monument to the earliest years of Christianity in England.

45

St Peter and St Paul, Salle, Norfolk
15th century

TG 110249. 1½ miles (2.4 km) NE of Reepham and N of B1145 Reepham to Cawston road

[C]

St Peter and St Paul, even more than most Norfolk churches, has a solitary setting and an atmosphere of timeless stillness. It stands out in open country with only a little Gothick school room for company, a strangely incongruous

setting for a building of such grandeur and nobility. Closely dateable to the first half of the 15th century, it was built as an expression of piety by patrons grown rich on wool. Thomas Rose, builder of the north transept, was prosecuted in 1425 for grazing 500 sheep on Cawston common where there should only have been 200. He and other wealthy donors are commemorated by numerous handsome brasses.

An exaggeratedly tall and slender tower resulted from the addition of an extra stage in the late 15th century. Calling to its neighbour Cawston St Agnes across the fields, it soars above the nave, dominating the exterior. The west door with its pair of censing angels, bears the arms of Henry V. The plan is unusually splendid, with north and south transepts and a pair of exceptional two-storey porches, which are vaulted at both levels, and originally housed a chapel and treasury.

The first impression of the interior is one of unencumbered space and soft ochre walls, suffused with mellow light. The simple, elegant lines of the arcade are carried up into the arch braced roof, which bears traces of painted decoration and carved angels. There is none of the magnificent exuberance of the hammerbeam roof of Cawston, but a gentler architectural unity. A resounding clunking announces the presence of a great clock on the medieval gallery in the tower, from which the tall and spiky font cover is suspended on a huge bracket. Mutilated by the removal of saints' images, it crowns a Seven Sacrament font (an East Anglian speciality) bearing an inscription to the donor, Thomas Luce (d.1489).

Further investigation reveals delicately carved roofs and an uncommonly complete ensemble of contemporary fittings: traceried doors with rare ironwork; a family pew made from painted panels; great carved bosses and fragments of rich Norwich School stained glass. A medieval wineglass pulpit, converted as a gift of Sir Thomas Knyvet in 1611 to a three-decker with a tester, was one of the very first examples of that type. The chancel arch with its painted screen dado is flanked by caryatid corbels which carried the beam on which the Great Rood, or Crucifixion, stood beneath the canopy of honour. Backing onto the screen is a fine set of stalls for the priests that served the guilds and chantries, with cowled heads as armrests, and carved misericords.

Salle is a quiet place, for solitary reflection and drinking in the atmosphere of one of Norfolk's loveliest churches.

46
Unitarian Meeting House, Ipswich, Suffolk
1699–1700

TM 162444. Friars Street, Ipswich town centre

[C]

In 1722 Daniel Defoe wrote that the Meeting House in Ipswich was 'as large and fine a building of that kind as most on this side of England, and the inside is the best finished of any I have seen, London not excepted . . .' Surviving virtually unaltered, it remains one of the finest of its date in the country.

Built for Presbyterians in 1699–1700 by the carpenter Joseph Clarke, the Meeting House maintained a discreet location set back from the street in a peaceful yard. Now in bizarre juxtaposition with modern architecture, it is reflected in the svelte black glass skin of the Willis Corroon Building (73, S), but holds its own against such competition. It has a robust and prosperous air, with vigorous classical detailing, but is not unsophisticated. A big, overhanging hipped roof with a chunky modillion cornice protects the plastered walls. A pair of wide, pedimented doors form the main entrance to Friars Street, with superb brackets, carved with cherubs' heads and doves, a curiously playful motif for a respectable Protestant building.

Unitarian Meeting House, Ipswich, the pulpit. RCHME

Two tiers of leaded cross casement windows and great oval *oeil-de-boeuf* light the rich interior of the building. As the form of Presbyterian worship centred on preaching, so the meeting-house interior focuses on the sumptuous double-decker pulpit with its gorgeous carved swags and barley sugar balusters. From this elevated position, the minister can survey his whole flock in their high box-pews or gallery benches. Giant columns support the wide span ceiling, from the centre of which hangs the splendid three-tiered brass chandelier, that lit the interior Defoe saw on his travels.

Plate 1   *Grimes Graves.* EH

Plate 2   *Framlingham Castle.* EH

Plate 3 *Castle Acre Priory.* EH

Plate 4   *The Memorial Chapel, American Military Cemetery, Madingley.* ABMC

Plate 5   *Chappel Viaduct by E R Smythe.*
IBCMG

Plate 6 *Willis Corroon building, Ipswich.* RCHME

Plate 7 *Entrance Hall, Holkham Hall.* AFK

Plate 8 (Right) *Statue of Diana, St Paul's Walden Bury.* JB

Plate 9 (Below) *The Great Court, Trinity College, Cambridge.* JB

Plate 10 (Right) *King's College Chapel, Cambridge, with Henry VIII's screen.* JB

Plate 11   *Stained glass, Holy Trinity, Long Melford.* AFK

Plate 12   *Cow Tower, Norwich.* JB

Plate 13   *Blickling Hall, south front.* NT

5

Public Buildings

Public, semi-public, educational and institutional buildings, and buildings for leisure and entertainment, take many forms in the region.

For centuries the Church was responsible for most education, hospitals, spiritual welfare, and births, deaths and marriages. Charity was dispensed from monasteries all over England. There were five medieval hospitals at Bury St Edmunds (S), one at each gate into the town. At Norwich (97, N) was the Great Hospital where the sick and poor were ministered to. The Dissolution of the Monasteries meant that greater provision for the needy began to fall on secular hands.

The Earl of Suffolk built an almshouse at Audley End (E) in the late 16th century. The pious Earl of Northampton endowed one at Castle Rising (N) in 1614 and Bishop Seth Ward founded **Ward's Hospital, Buntingford** (53, H) in 1684. In 1702 the Corporation of Great Yarmouth (N) founded the lovely 'Hospital for Decayed Fishermen'. There are other good examples from the 18th century at St Albans (H), Dunstable (B) and Ampthill (B). The inhabitants of these places were fortunate compared with many and the problem of housing increasing numbers of poor grew until workhouses were introduced in the late 18th century.

Early workhouses like **Gressenhall** (50, N), Hales (N) and Stowmarket (S) were 'paupers' palaces' built along domestic Georgian lines. After 1834 there was a workhouse boom and numerous grim examples were put up, often to designs by keen young architects like G G Scott. One of his buildings survives at Great Dunmow (E). Many workhouses were in use until the mid-20th century. The laws which sent people to these wretched places were upheld in local court rooms like that preserved at the Shire Hall, Little Walsingham (N). Here, justice was dispensed, often leading to sentences served in prisons such as Little

Walsingham's Bridewell, or the Old Gaol, Bury St Edmunds (S).

Civic activities took place in 15th-century guildhalls in Norwich and **Thaxted** (51, E) and shire halls like that at Woodbridge (S; of 1575). Local government offices proliferated in the 18th and 19th centuries: Bedford Town Hall (B) and Chelmsford Shire Hall (E) being typical of many throughout the country. Eye (S) has E B Lamb's roguish town hall, covered in flint like hundreds and thousands; **Colchester Town Hall** (48, E) is High Victorian and splendid; Norwich City Hall, built in the 1930s and Swedish-inspired, dominates the city centre.

Education is well represented in the region. Colleges were founded in Cambridge (93, N) in the 13th century and grew through many changes into a great university. Grammar and public schools founded by bishops, wealthy merchants or companies, flourished from the mid-16th century onwards. Berkhamsted School (H) dates from the 1540s, Haileybury College (H) from 1809. Haileybury belonged to the East India Company, who employed William Wilkins as their architect. He gave the College a grand portico and a dome. Royal Hospital School, Holbrook (S), built in the 1920s, is impressively scaled, with a Wren-inspired steeple. Henry Morris tried to stir life into rural Cambridgeshire with the village colleges, of which **Impington Village College** (52, C), designed by Modern Movement architects in the 1930s, is the best. After the Second World War, Hertfordshire County Council led the whole country with their programme of light, colourful and cheap-to-build schools. There were good ones at Essendon (H), Stevenage (H) and Cheshunt (H). Alison and Peter Smithson went further; Hunstanton Secondary Modern School (N) was passionately plain in 1953, its function and materials expressed with ruthless honesty. In the 1960s two new

The Fishermen's Hospital, Great Yarmouth. AFK

universities were founded in the region: the University of Essex at Colchester (E) and, in Norwich, the University of East Anglia which attracted much publicity for its stepped pyramid blocks and, later, its high-tech Sainsbury Centre.

Cemeteries and war memorials belong largely to the 19th and 20th centuries. The Nelson Column, Great Yarmouth, of 1817, is a reminder of the Napoleonic Wars. Almost every town and village has its Great War memorial, in church, churchyard, or other public place. The wider conflict of the Second World War is represented by the crisply landscaped **American Military Cemetery** near Cambridge (47, C).

Places for entertainment and leisure must begin with inns, of which the Red Lion, Colchester (E) is a heavily timbered example dating from c.1500. The Duke's Head Inn, King's Lynn (94, N) was built by Henry Bell in the late 17th century. The Angel Hotel, Bury St Edmunds, is mentioned in Dickens's *Pickwick Papers*. There are big 19th-century hotels in seaside towns like Great Yarmouth, Cromer (N) and **Southwold** (99, S). Until recently there were no end of traditional pubs which were well supplied by local breweries.

In large towns, provincial theatres and assembly rooms entertained the local gentry in the late 18th and early

19th centuries. Bury St Edmunds has an Athenaeum and a rare Georgian playhouse, the Theatre Royal. Later there were Great Yarmouth's glazed-in Winter Gardens and its purpose-built circus, the Hippodrome. In the early 20th century cinemas appeared, like the **Electric Palace Cinema, Harwich** (49, E). Open-air swimming pools, funfairs and piers are coastal specialities. Hunstanton, Great Yarmouth and Clacton (E) all have noteworthy piers, and Southend (E) has the longest pier in the world.

47

American Military Cemetery, Madingley, Cambridgeshire
20th century

TL 402596. 2 miles (3.2 km) W of Cambridge off A1303

[C]

This is a solemn and scenic place. Solemn, because this is a memorial to 8,936 Americans who were killed in the Second World War. Scenic, because it commands distant views across the flat lands of Cambridgeshire.

The cemetery was established in 1943 and dedicated in 1956. Its landscaping and buildings were carried out by American architects. A belt of trees separates the cemetery from the road. There is a simple visitors' building at the entrance. A tall flagpole marks one end of the Great Mall and at the other end stands the Memorial Chapel. In between there are pools of still water and, running alongside, a paved terrace and the Wall of the Missing on which 5,125 names are inscribed. On this Wall there are four statues representing each arm of the United States forces: soldier, sailor, airman, coast guardsman. The chapel bears a huge stone relief map of the British Isles on the outside of its south wall. This shows the location of all American wartime bases. Teak entrance doors carry bronze models of vehicles and ships. Further modelling is found inside the chapel. Another large stone map of Europe and the Atlantic dominates the single room. From across

56

American Military Cemetery, Madingley. ABMC

the sea and from Britain radiate small
metal models of ships and aircraft. The
effect of these gold and silver symbols is
strangely moving. They portray the
'Great Air Assault' on enemy-occupied
Europe. Blue, white and gold mosaic
covers the ceiling, a poignant memorial
to those who lost their lives in the skies
over Germany. Convoys of aircraft
escorted by angels are depicted flying
eastwards towards the light.

On the north side of the Great Mall
3,811 graves with white crosses and
Stars of David fan out across immaculate
lawns. Everything here is crisply
detailed and well ordered. Trim box-
wood hedges divide the grave plots.
Shrubs border the far side of the lawns.
Far away in the distance looms Ely
Cathedral (21, C), a once familiar
landmark for many who lie buried here
amidst firethorn, liquidambar and
mournful Rose of Sharon.

48

Colchester Town Hall, Essex
1898–1902

TL 995253. In Colchester High
Street, town centre

[D]

A show-off of a building, nicknamed
Belchester after its expansive architect
John Belcher. He won the competition
to provide Colchester with a new Town

Hall, and produced this splendid High
Victorian baroque piece in 1898–1902.
Built in brick, with lashings of stone it is
an Imperial-looking pile with echoes of
17th-century palaces and churches. The
whole building is electrifyingly self-
possessed; the part it plays in the
townscape superbly managed.

The main facade has a heavily
rusticated ground floor which acts as a
plinth for three pairs of giant composite
columns. These carry broken pediments,
triangular in the centre, segmental on
either side. There are tall windows with
delicate glazing bars, rather demure-
looking, amidst the bulging, pushing-

Colchester Town Hall, the tower. From *The Builder*, 24 December 1898. RCHME

and-shoving scrolls, balconies and heraldic sculpture. The main theme is lifted from Hawksmoor's Greenwich Palace, the bravura treatment of details and decoration plundered from Wren's St Paul's Cathedral and Hampton Court. But this is not mere copyism. It is a brilliant freewheeling reinterpretation and something to be savoured. The tower is a stupefying mixture of Wren's city churches and Borromini's Roman baroque. It is 162 ft (49.3 m) high and is placed for maximum effect, where the street begins to narrow. Belchester's interiors are hardly less impressive: on the ground floor there are spacious offices; on the first floor, which Belcher treated as a piano nobile, are the Council Chamber and the Mayor's Parlour; on the floor above, a large room for public meetings. The Council Chamber has especially fine decorations, handled more lightly than the outside of the building might suggest.

Turn-of-the-century baroque was in great demand for public and government buildings. It suggested authority and opulence. It could be done ponderously or, as here, with panache. As well as an architect, Belcher was a talented musician and conductor. Colchester Town Hall is his masterpiece: 'Pomp and Circumstance' in D major, with the whole orchestra fighting mad.

49

Electric Palace Cinema, Harwich, Essex
1911

TM 261326. Kings Quay Street, Harwich
[C]

The Electric Palace Cinema is a remarkable survival. This purpose-built silent screen cinema, after closing its doors for the last time in 1956, had been locked up and forgotten, only to be 'rediscovered' in 1972 with the tickets still in the pay box and films in the projection room. Dating from 1911, it was not one of the earliest cinemas, which were already being built in large numbers from 1905, but it is now

Electric Palace Cinema, Harwich. P ROGERS/ECC

certainly the most complete. David Atwell described it in his *Cathedrals of the Movies* (1980) as 'the rarest and most precious survival in England'.

The cinema was designed by the young Ipswich architect Harold Hooper for the celebrated Charles Thurston, a travelling fairground showman, and was built at a cost of £1,500. Wednesday, 29 November 1911, the opening night, offered an exciting programme of films including *The Battle of Trafalgar* and the *Death of Nelson*; *The Cowboy's Devotedness*; *Harry the Footballer* and a number of short supporting comedies. Naturally, they were accompanied by a pianist in the pit, with appropriate sound effects from the wings. In the early years vaudeville acts often formed a major part of the entertainment, and the dressing rooms beneath the small stage have survived. In 1930, a little later than elsewhere, the talkies came to Harwich in the form of Al Jolson's *The Singing Fool* and still in place in 1972 were the primitive sound horns installed for that performance.

The cheerful Edwardian baroque facade, with its open-fronted entrance lobby and paired doors flanking the

charming timber ticket kiosk, was executed in a slightly modified form to the surviving plans of 1911. Inside, the auditorium with its shallow barrel vault and ornate plaster decoration is of the same period. On the rear wall of the stage is the original plaster screen, later superseded by a canvas screen which hung behind the proscenium arch.

Thanks to the efforts of a dedicated group of volunteers who repaired and re-opened the cinema and now run it as a charitable Trust, visitors can once more experience the thrill of entering the dimmed auditorium in anticipation of another performance at England's finest 'Picture Palace'.

50

Gressenhall Workhouse, Norfolk
18th–19th century

TF 975171. 3½ miles (5.6 km) N of East Dereham off B1146
[A]

'Paupers' palaces', or workhouses, were landmarks in eastern England. Sited on he edge of towns or in open countryside, they were purpose-built complexes where the ill, aged, orphaned, and the general poor could be housed, fed and employed. Workhouses were a response to the breakdown of the old Elizabethan system which made parishes responsible for poor relief. From the mid-18th century onwards parishes began to group together to fund these necessarily large buildings.

Gressenhall Workhouse was built in 1776–7 on the site of an old farm. It is a plain brick building with extended wings and white painted windows. The symmetrical facade, central pediment and rooftop cupola, place it firmly in the English classical tradition of rather simple country mansions. This was not a grim joke: the Georgians saw no contradiction in making warehouses, mills, breweries and other workaday buildings conform to accepted ideas of architectural taste.

Between 450 and 670 paupers lived at Gressenhall, and to begin with the regime was not harsh. On a typical summer's day work started at 6.00 a.m. with breakfast for half-an-hour at 8.00 a.m., then work until 12.00 p.m. There was one-and-a-half hours for dinner and rest, and then work again until 6.00 p.m. when supper was served. Bedtime was at 9.00 p.m. In winter the timetable was only slightly different. The able-bodied worked in the fields, and at weaving, spinning and domestic chores. Residents could keep some of the money they earned. There was education for children and no unnecessary discipline. Food was plentiful but dull.

The 1834 Poor Law Amendment Act changed all that. Workhouses began to resemble prisons; poverty became almost a crime. Conditions were made as miserable as possible in order to reduce expenses and keep any but the most desperate away.

At Gressenhall these changes were reflected by the introduction of a hard, punitive regime, which at times came close to the sadistic cruelty of *Oliver Twist*. Walls went up; young married couples were separated; meals were eaten in silence; offenders punished in the 'refractory cell'. Old married couples were treated a little better: if well behaved they were shoved off to Cherry Tree Cottage. Towards the end of the 19th century there was some relaxing of workhouse strictness. But the imagery and fear of 'the workshouse' remained until the creation of the Welfare State after the Second World War.

Gressenhall is now a Museum of Rural Life and its buildings and exhibits are open to the public. Some of the bleak atmosphere has been retained on purpose, but the paupers' graveyard has become a picnic area.

51
Guildhall, Thaxted, Essex
c.*1450*

TL 611309. Thaxted, 6 miles (9.6 km) SE of Saffron Walden. In town centre, on B184

[C]

The three-tiered Guildhall, standing at the head of Thaxted Market Place with the transcendent form of the church rising above it, is one of the most satisfying townscape vistas in Essex. Behind it, a jumble of overhanging timber-framed houses winds up the cobbled Stoney Lane to the churchyard gate.

The Guildhall was built in 1430–60 (as determined by tree-ring dating), at which time the town was thriving on profits from the cutlery industry. The Essex historian Morant, writing in 1768, described the building as the 'Gild or Motehall'. Tradition states that it was built for the 'Cutlers' Guild', but in fact this guild probably never existed in medieval Thaxted. There were at least three religious guilds in the town but craft guilds as such were known only in major cities. During the Reformation, religious guilds were disbanded and many of their halls were converted to houses and shops or demolished. This

Gressenhall Workhouse, now the Rural Life Museum. NMS

59

Thaxted Guildhall. JC

52
Impington Village College, Cambridgeshire
1938

TL 447632. In New Road, Impington [D]

building had probably always doubled as a Market Cross and so continued in use, the upper floor becoming the Moot Hall.

The timber superstructure, built over a brick and flint cellar, is constructed around a massive central post from which diagonal dragon beams run out to support the jetty running around three sides. This bold and dramatic design is cleverly adapted to the site, making it the focal point of the market place. The open arcaded ground floor, probably used as a market hall, has a room above lit by a continuous band of unglazed windows with shutters. The two top-floor rooms were lit by large oriel windows.

At first the Guildhall was crowned by twin gables adorned, no doubt, with elaborately carved bargeboards. When, in 1714, it became a grammar school, the gables were changed to hips and it was 'improved' to modern standards of comfort and fashion by plastering over the exposed timber work and inserting leaded-light casement windows. A new staircase and town lock-up were built against the rear wall and fireplaces and panelling were put in. In 1911 the process was reversed by the woodcarver Ernest Beckwith, who had previously restored Paycockes Coggeshall (E). His

aim, controversial even then, was to return the building to 'its ancient form, going behind the vandalism of the Georgian period'. He duly stripped off the plaster, put back 'medieval' style windows and replaced with plain braces the delicate ogee arches of the arcade, mistakenly believing them to be 18th century. A delightful palimpsest of a building, the Guildhall warns of the perils of taking old buildings at face value.

'One of the best buildings of its date in England, if not the best.' That was Pevsner's opinion of Impington Village College. Those clean, elegant lines, cheerful colours, well-planned rooms and large windows were as fresh as fresh air in 1938. The architects were Maxwell Fry and Walter Gropius, the international 'star' and pioneer of the Modern Movement. The ideas behind the architecture were those of Henry Morris, County Education Secretary for Cambridgeshire in the 1930s.

Henry Morris was an extraordinary man. A reformer and a socialist, an aesthete and a lover of Italy, a contradictory and often unpopular figure, Morris was a man with vision. His vision was to revitalise a long neglected rural England through a system of village colleges. Morris's ideas were radical. He wanted more and better education for children, and continuing education and recreational opportunities for adults. He believed that architecture held many of the answers to these social needs. 'Every

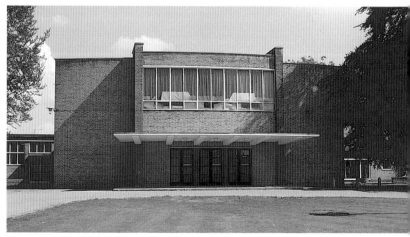

Impington Village College. NC

own and every village must have its educational buildings' declared Morris. The village college with its combination of classrooms, community facilities, clinic, and shared library and hall, set amongst trees and lawns was to be the fulfilment of the social mission. Cambridgeshire County Council bravely went ahead and built some village colleges.

Sawston (1927–30) was fashionable (and dull) neo-Georgian; Bottisham and Linton (1937–8) were unhistorical and Dutch-inspired; Impington was revolutionary; a touch of the Bauhaus amidst the cabbage fields of Cambridgeshire. England's 19th- and early 20th-century educational buildings were often pompous, desperate places, designed 'by rote' and no joy to work in. Impington was a new model school; relaxed, practical, at the same time ambitious. It was built on old parkland and the architects deliberately took advantage of mature trees, fitting the buildings between them. Building materials were straightforward; local rough-textured bricks, steel windows, timber roofs covered with boarding and asphalt. Interiors were of light grey brick, pointed with yellow cement. The plan involved a loose but sensitively worked out arrangement of rooms, the most striking of which was the fan-shaped hall with its projecting walls and tall windows. To the left of this ran the adult wing, a single-storey range with bright bay windows. Behind the hall was the main concourse around which everything else was grouped. It was all very novel, enlightened and un-traditional. Despite later additions the essential design is still clear.

To understand why Impington was so pioneering in the late 1930s requires seeing it through new eyes, forgetting much of what has happened in the past fifty years. Fry and Gropius were the first modern architects to build a school in England and it was Impington's architecture and not the ideals it stood for which was so admired and influential after the Second World War. When the ideals finally took shape in the community comprehensive schools of the 1960s and 1970s the village England which Morris had wanted to serve was dead. His hope that a new series of worthy public buildings would 'stand side by side with the parish churches of the countryside' was never realised.

53

Ward's Hospital, Buntingford, Hertfordshire
17th century

TL 363295. In High Street, Buntingford

[D]

In the 16th and 17th centuries private individuals often built almshouses for the aged and the poor. These served as handy memorials to their founders who might be merchants, rising gentlemen or bishops. Types of 17th-century almshouses vary from a simple row of cottages, like Wynne's in Baldock (H) to a courtyard arrangement like the Duchess of Marlborough's almshouses, St Albans (H). The type achieved its finest expression in Christopher Wren's Chelsea Hospital, London.

Ward's Hospital is a good example of the small three-sided courtyard plan almshouse. It was founded in 1684 by Seth Ward, Bishop of Salisbury who, according to the inscription above the central doorway, was born in Buntingford and educated in 'ye free-skool' there. This doorway has a swan-neck pediment and shield bearing Bishop Ward's arms. Above, a small triangular pediment emphasises the symmetry of the almshouse. The whole building is of local red brick and tile, dressed with white stone. Well proportioned, with unfussy architectural details, each separate dwelling has its own doorway and plain mullioned windows. A low wall with railings encloses the forecourt-cum-garden.

The architect of this charming composition is not known, but it could have been Dr Robert Hooke, designer of Wren lookalikes, inventor of microscopes and of 'thirty severall wayes of Flying'. His most famous building was the palace-sized London madhouse called 'Bedlam'.

Seth Ward endowed another rather beautiful almshouse in Salisbury, Wiltshire, but it is his Buntingford 'Hospital' which represents one of the purest moments in the almshouse tradition and is also a fine example of 'local boy makes good and comes home to show off'. The almshouse stands back from the road and groups with a rare early 17th-century Greek-cross plan church. The south range of the almshouse nudges right up to the church, leaving only a narrow passage between them. There is a comfortable relationship of scale and materials, and a visual harmony between the two buildings; a modest piece of 17th-century planning which still works surprisingly well.

6

Agriculture and Industry

Agriculture was and is the main industry of the region. The landscape is man-made to a greater extent than in most other parts of England. In the Middle Ages sheep farming and its related woollen cloth trade flourished. Grain production accounts for the numerous huge barns, such as the 13th-century **Cressing Temple Barns** (56, E) and the 16th-century **Waxham Great Barn** (62, N) which are such a feature of the region. In the 16th century Essex was known as the 'Englishe Goshen' a land of plenty, with prosperous farmers and merchants. Essex farmsteads often took the form of moated sites with farmhouse, barns, granary and dovecote. Few dovecotes are as impressive as the one at **Willington** (57, B). Farms were small by modern standards, but by the 17th century Norfolk and Suffolk were exporting corn, livestock and poultry in ever-increasing quantities.

Vermuyden's draining of the Fens in the mid-17th century had far-reaching effects. It led to the formation of huge tracts of the richest farmland in Europe; it destroyed the way of life of the fen-dwelling 'Slodgers' and created a draining, dyking, water-pumping industry of its own. **Stretham Old Engine** (61, C) Denver Sluice (N) and numerous straight channels and rivers are impressive relics of that industry.

In the Agricultural Revolution, which began in the late 18th century, the progressive gentry of eastern England led the way. Coke of Holkham, 'Turnip' Townshend and the Dukes of Bedford amongst others experimented, planned and wrote about farming. Crop rotations, new grasses and clovers, cattle fodder and improvements in farm management all came from the eastern counties, Norfolk in particular. Model farms with specialised buildings were built at Woburn (B), Wimpole (C) and Holkham (N). **Wimpole Home Farm** (63, C) was largely designed by Soane. The Great Barn at Holkham evoked the grandeur of Rome.

Amongst agriculture-related industries, malting, brewing and milling have left the most remains. By the 19th century most of England's barley was grown in the eastern counties. Maltings were found everywhere: on riverside sites in small market towns like Bishop's Stortford (H), Hertford (H) and Stowmarket (S); at quaysides in Mistley (E), Ipswich (S) and King's Lynn (94, N); alongside railway lines in Bury St Edmunds (S) and Beccles (S). Their tall kilns, brick or weatherboarded malting floors and low slatted windows are fine examples of the functional tradition. Breweries were widespread and ranged in size from 'one man' brewing sheds to bigger sites like Adnams in Southwold (99, S), Ridley's, near Felsted (E) and Elgoods in Wisbech (C), all of which are still producing beer.

A regional speciality was the silk industry which developed after refugee weavers fled to England from the Continent in the late 17th century. White, weatherboarded silk mills from the industry's later period can be found in the Essex towns of Halstead (E), Braintree (E) and Bocking (E). In the 1830s the Norwich Yarn Company built a splendid and simple brick mill beside the River Wensum in Norwich (97, N).

Watermills and windmills are the classic rural industrial buildings of the region. They were built to grind flour for bread, to power farm machinery, or to drain low-lying fields in the Broads or Fens. Most rivers had watermills and many survive; brick-built in Norfolk, timber-framed and weatherboarded in Essex, Hertfordshire and Suffolk. Coggeshall (E), Stebbing (E) and Sible Hedingham (E) have interesting examples. **Woodbridge** (64, S) has a rare tide-mill. Constable made Flatford Mill (S) famous.

Windmills are familiar shapes on the eastern skyline. Post mills have black or white wooden bodies usually mounted above a brick roundhouse like those at Aythorpe Roding (E) and **Saxtead Green**

Saxtead Green Post Mill. EH

Fen drains at Angle Corner, Whittlesey. DP

(60, S). Tower mills are tall brick towers with a cap carrying the sails on top. Stansted Mountfitchet (E) has a slender one, Thaxted (E) a fat one. Drainage windmills look very similar, but their main function was to pump water. The Broads are dotted with their remains. **Berney Arms Windmill** (55, N) is a carefully restored example. The small wooden smock mill at Wicken Fen (C) represents another once very common type of drainage mill.

Limited water-power and a lack of raw materials and fossil fuels combined with the remote geography of its eastern parts to ensure that little heavy industry

developed in the region. Agriculture was predominant and engineering firms like Garretts of Leiston and Savages of King's Lynn served its needs, building threshing machines and steam engines and forging all kinds of implements. Today the premises built for Garretts are a museum, the **Leiston Long Shop** (59, S) being an exceptionally early example of an 'assembly line' building.

Extractive industries included flint mining at Grimes Graves (4, N), one of the oldest industrial sites in England; nearby Brandon (S) became a centre for flint knapping. There was a small amount of quarrying for limestone, carstone and brick clay. Brick making was an early activity. By the 19th century it had become and has remained a major industry in Bedfordshire and Cambridgeshire.

Public service industries included the supply of water and gas. The New River Company sent water from Hertfordshire to London along an artificial canal cut in the 17th century; a landscaped section at **Amwell Pool, Great Amwell** (54, H) is still operational. Nearby there is a Victorian pumping station from a later phase in the industry's development.

Small town gasworks were common from the mid-19th century onwards but **Fakenham Gasworks** (58, N) is now preserved as the last surviving example in England.

Specialist and domestic industries once proliferated. Along the coast fishing was important and Great Yarmouth (N) and Lowestoft (S) became fish exporting ports, the latter well served by railways. In Bedfordshire straw-plaiting, straw-hatting and lacemaking flourished. Airships were built at Cardington (67, B) and aircraft at Hatfield (H). Hertfordshire's lesser known industries included paper and gunpowder manufacture, sheepdip, fireworks, herbs and Hitch's patent interlocking bricks. Everywhere there were coopers, carpenters, ironmongers, tanners and builders; their humble yards and workshops still add scale and dignity to many of the region's towns and villages.

54

Amwell Pool, Great Amwell, and the New River, Hertfordshire
17th–19th century

TL 372126. In Amwell Lane, Great Amwell, 1½ miles (2.4 km) off A10(T) E of Hertford
[C]

The New River takes 'sweete' water into London. It is an artificial channel which was originally fed by springs in Chadwell (H) and Great Amwell (H) before meandering for 40 miles (64.3 km) to New River Head in Islington, London. Today the New River carries water from the River Lea, near Ware (H) to Stoke Newington reservoirs, in the London Borough of Hackney. The idea for the New River was taken up by Hugh Myddleton, MP, alderman and goldsmith, who got the project started, kept it going in the face of City opposition, and ambitiously part-financed it himself. It was cut in 1609–13 and was immediately popular with those wealthy enough to have the fresh water piped into their homes.

Stewartby brickworks, worked-out claypit with kiln chimneys beyond. BCC

1830. By then water was already being drawn from the River Lea via a special intake gauge.

A short way along the river bank east of Emma's Well stands Amwell Marsh pumping station, one of several built in the late 19th century to assist in coping with London's insatiable demand for water. The pumps drew water up from purpose-dug wells. Amwell Marsh was built in Italianate fancy dress in 1884. The attendant's cottage stands next door. Municipal style railings, drab notices and trim are 20th-century contributions to Amwell Pool. They do not intrude too much; water and trees still 'delight the eye and refresh the spirit'.

55

Berney Arms Windmill, Norfolk
19th century

TG 465049. 3½ miles (5.6 km) NE of Reedham. Accessed by train (no road access): alight at Berney Arms Halt and follow footpath to windmill. Also accessible by water

[A] EH

Windmill and winding river, fields dotted with cattle, remote railway halt; Berney Arms is a Broadland place of simple beauty. Situated in the Halvergate Marshes, access by car is impractical, though there is an infrequent train service from Norwich or Yarmouth. The mill is a tapering black tower with white sails, built by Stolworthy's of Yarmouth sometime after 1850. It stands close to the River Yare, and served a dual purpose: to lift flood water out of the fields and meadows and to grind cement clinker. Once there were many such 'marsh mills' at work draining the Broads. The typical form was a brick tower with a wooden cap carrying sails which provided power to drive a scoopwheel enclosed in a ground-level wooden extension or hoodway. There are examples at Horsey (N), Stracey Arms (N) and Thurne Dyke (N), and smaller ones elsewhere on the Broads. Berney

Amwell Pool, Great Amwell. PDB

Myddleton took the credit and gained a knighthood for his trouble.

At Great Amwell, where the second of the feeder springs rose, the water channel broadens to form a shady pool. There are two green-edged islands planted with yew and weeping willow, and a backdrop of trees rising to a hill with a medieval church upon it. This miniature piece of picturesque landscaping was carried out by Robert Mylne, Chief Engineer to the New River Company at the turn of the 18th century. His original scheme took in River Cottage and the grounds of Amwell Grove, his own house. The two

islands have ornamental urns placed upon them. The largest urn, a tasteful piece of Coade stone, was put there by Mylne in 1800. Its pedestal is inscribed to the 'Genius, Talents and elevation of mind' of Sir Hugh Myddleton. There is some free-flowing Latin on two other sides, and Mylne thoughtfully added his own name in big letters. The urn on the smaller island, inscribed with some second-rate poetry, was put up in 1818. On the north-east side of the pool, across the lane, is Emma's Well, now a brick-lined basin full of leaves. This was one of the sources of the New River, although its spring dried up around

65

Berney Arms Windmill. EH

Arms is the tallest at seven storeys, 70 ft (21.3 m) high. Its big scoopwheel is mounted in a semi-circular hoodway beside the mill. This is linked by two shafts, one horizontal, the other vertical, to the sail gearing inside the cap.

The cap is mounted on an iron track and the sails are turned into the wind by means of the fantail. Grinding machinery was originally housed on the various diminishing-sized floors, although these are now creaking and empty. Plain wooden ladders link each floor. Small-paned windows allow snatched views of the landscape outside.

Until replaced by electric plant, drainage mills were identified in a particular way with the marshy landscape of the Broads. Painted black and white and often given boat-shaped caps, their firm, clear outlines were unmistakable. Berney Arms is the finest of them to have survived. Its sails still turn in the wind; a sight, R L Stevenson warned, which provokes such pleasure in a visitor that ever afterwards 'wind-mills keep turning up in his dreams'.

56
Cressing Temple Barns, Essex
13th century

TL 799188. 3 miles (4.8 km) N of Witham off B1018

[A]

In 1137, Queen Matilda granted the manor of Cressing to the recently

founded military order of The Knights of the Temple. Based in Jerusalem, these professional knights lived under monastic rule and were dedicated to protecting Christian pilgrims to the Holy Land. Fighting the Infidel under the banner of the Croix Rouge (Red Cross), the Templars captured the imagination of Europe's nobility in the grip of Crusading fervour. Many rich estates were showered on them and they were granted exemption from all but papal authority.

Cressing was one of the earliest of the order's fifty or so principal estates in England, profits from which were channelled overseas to support the fighting forces. Cressing had its own chapel, but in other respects resembled a grand secular manor. An inventory made in 1313 describes its hall-house, kitchen, brewhouse and dairy with a small granary, cider mill and smithy. Central to the farming operations of any estate were the great barns, into which was loaded the harvested crop for threshing, before the grain was transferred to the granary for storage. The two magnificent barns in the northern corner of the moated site at Cressing are the best preserved timber examples of their date and provide vivid testimony to the wealth of the Templars, being the sole surviving buildings from their time on the site.

The Wheat Barn, tree-ring dated to c.1250–80, is the more complete of the two and gives the best impression of early medieval carpentry, characterised by the use of very long, straight, square section oak timbers. The aisled structure

uses lap joints and is braced by long secondary rafters, or passing braces, which run parallel with the roof from the outer walls, crossing just below the apex. The same system of bracing was largely removed from the Barley Barn, of c.1200–30, when it was reduced in size and given a crown post roof in the 15th century, but the central trusses show the heavily timbered construction with paired tie beams and cross bracing.

The fortunes of the Knights Templars waned with those of the Crusading movement after the Fall of Acre in 1291, and the order was finally dissolved in 1312 under accusations of heresy, blasphemy and devil worship. Cressing, with the rest of the English estates, was transferred, after extensive asset stripping by the Crown, to the Knights of the Order of St John, or Hospitallers. After the Dissolution the site passed to the Smith family who erected a 'greate house' which disappeared in the 18th century, leaving a large granary, sometime used as a courthall, the walled garden and farmhouse.

57
Dovecote and Stables, Willington, Bedfordshire
16th century

TL 107499. 4 miles (6.4 km) E of Bedford off A603 Sandy Road, from which site is signposted

[B] NT

Sir John Gostwick, MP, High Sheriff and Master of the Horse to Henry VIII, built

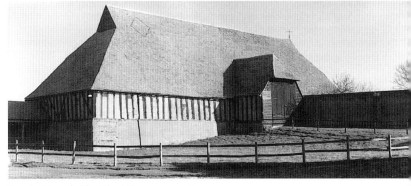

Cressing Temple, the Wheat Barn. P ROGERS/ECC

Willington Dovecote. AFK

58

Fakenham Gasworks, Norfolk
19th–20th century

TF 919293. In Hempton Road,
Fakenham

[A]

In 1805 Pall Mall in London became the
first street in the world to be lit by gas.
By the end of the century there were
hundreds of gasworks scattered
throughout the cities, towns and villages
of England. Now there is only one.
Fakenham gasworks is the last example
of a small country gasworks in England.
'Fakenham has just been lighted by gas',
reported the *Norwich Mercury* on 21
November 1846. The buildings of this
hand-worked gasworks date from then
and with modifications and occasional
renewal of plant they supplied the
market town with gas until 1965.

Fakenham gasworks was sited at the
lowest part of the town (because gas
rises) close to the railway station which
supplied it with coal. Despite their
unsavoury reputation small gasworks
were part of the day-to-day life of a
country town. As well as gas they
produced tar and coke which were sold
as by-products. Even the all-pervasive
iron oxide smell had a use; it was a
popular cure for whooping cough.
Mothers pushed their prams into the
gasworks; small children with sore
throats spluttered in the street outside.

Gasworks were traditionally untidy
places; a jumble of buildings, pipes and
equipment that was generally reckoned
to be unsightly and rough. This packed-
in, backyard flavour is well preserved at
Fakenham. There are exhausters,
purifiers, condenser, Livesey Washer,
oxide shed, station meter and booster
pump. Shifted off to one side is a cast-
iron, single lift gasholder of 1888.
Opposite is the retort house, a brick
building with a louvred roof, where coal
was burnt to produce crude gas. Inside is
a startling battery of black iron retorts,
or ovens. A stoker was in charge of these
and the work was filthy and unhealthy.
An 'Engineer and Manager' lived in the
cottage attached to the works. In its

a mansion on his newly acquired estate
at Willington during the 1530s. It has
long since vanished, leaving his
remarkable dovecote and stables
forlornly standing in a field. In the
church nearby, which Sir John rebuilt,
are his tomb and the helmet he wore at
the Field of the Cloth of Gold.

Silhouetted against the open sky, the
jagged outline of the great dovecote
resembles a Scottish tower house. Its
massive 3 ft (0.9 m) thick walls, built
with stone from Bedford and Newnham
priories, are pierced only by two
miniature doorways, giving it a fortified
air. Its romantic overtones were not out
of place, for the dovecote was a manorial
privilege as late as the 18th century, and
the meat was a delicacy restricted to the
tables of the rich.

In spite of its fanciful appearance, the
dovecote is in fact a highly functional
structure, specifically designed for its
purpose. The tiny doors allow a man
standing in the entrance to block it

completely, preventing the birds from
flying out. Louvres in the roof and the
single dormer provide ventilation and
access for the birds, whilst keeping out
larger birds of prey.

The crow-stepped gables are exploited
for maximum aesthetic impact and also
provide shelter and perches. In the
dimly lit interior, 1,500 nesting boxes
with alighting ledges line the walls.
A timber framework and ladder climb
to the upper levels to allow the
squabs, or young birds, to be collected
for eating.

The stable block, traditionally
another prestigious building reflecting
the importance of the riding horse, is
similarly untouched by any of the
Renaissance influences already
appearing in the 1520s, for example, at
Layer Marney Towers (83, E). This is of
an earlier age, a thoroughly Gothic
building, befitting a man who was a
player on the stage of the last great
pageant of the Middle Ages.

Fakenham Gasworks, view across the purifiers to the retort house. EH

heyday the gasworks employed eight men and had about 500 customers.

Electricity, nationalisation and North Sea gas put an end to small country gasworks. Fakenham's served its community well, adding scale, variety and interest to a drab part of town and sending a warm glow of light into streets and homes.

59
Leiston Long Shop, Suffolk
1852

TM 445626. Leiston, 3¼ miles (5.2 km) NW of Aldeburgh on B1122. In Main Street

[A]

Garretts of Leiston was a typical agricultural engineering firm. The firm began in 1778 as a small forge turning out farm implements: scythes, sickles, ploughs, harrows, seed-drills and ironmongery for estate gates and fences. In 1806 Garretts built their first wood and iron threshing machine. In 1851 they had a stand at the Great Exhibition and six years later were employing 500 men. As time went on their products got heavier and more varied: steamrollers, road locomotives and tractors, bakers' ovens, dough mixers, 'O'-type trolleybuses and dry-cleaning machines. They made 'Six Man Living Vans' for road works, vans for the Savoy Hotel Laundry, and much of the Never Stop Railway for the 1924 Wembley Exhibition.

For over 100 years Garretts and Leiston were inseparable. The works

formed an island site around which the village grew. There were workshops, water-towers, offices, housing for workers, a Hall and an Institute. Most important of all was the Long Shop. This tall brick building was put up in 1852. It has an iron and timber-framed gallery inside, creating a wide nave with side aisles, and was nicknamed 'the Cathedral'. Here steam engines were built on a production-line basis. Boilers were pulled in by horses at one end of the shop and moved along while parts were attached from the aisles or the gallery above. Overhead cranes were used for heavy lifting. Lighting was by gas produced by the firm's own gasworks. Small by modern standards, but simple and effective enough for its purpose, the Long Shop is one of the first flow-line assembly halls in the world.

In the 20th century, changing patterns of industry and employment affected Garretts and many similar East Anglian firms. The 1920s recession hit them badly and Garretts was bought out. The firm was re-started and continued in business until 1980 when it closed for good. Much of Garretts' original site has been altered or demolished but part, including the Long Shop, is now a museum. The cluster of buildings and

Traction engines at Leiston long shop. LONG SHOP MUSEUM

yards is crammed with goods made by Garretts ranging from iron hoes to ice-cream freezers. The atmosphere of a small town's engineering works still lingers. Occasionally an engine 'puk-puk-puks' into life in vivid demonstration of the wholesome power and smell of steam.

60
Saxtead Green Post Mill, Suffolk
1792

TM 253645. 2 miles (3.2 km) W of Framlingham

[A] EH

Saxtead Mill, built in 1792 is one of the finest windmills in England. It stands in gently rolling hedge-and-cornfield country in East Suffolk where the art of post-mill building reached perfection.

A post mill has a wooden buck or body carrying sails and milling machinery, which turns upon a central oak post. The post is anchored by cross-trees and is usually protected by a tarred or painted roundhouse, which is useful for storage. All these features are found at Saxtead, where the buck is reached by a giddy-making ladder supporting a fantail. The fantail helped turn the buck into the wind. No two post mills are ever exactly alike. There are subtle differences, but details like the handrail on the ladder or the shape of a porch or doorway are always simple and crisp.

Going inside Saxtead Mill is like going below deck on a windjammer. There are three storeys in the roundhouse, followed by three more in the buck. Headroom is limited and each floor is cluttered with equipment: complicated gear-wheels with hornbeam or apple cogs, heavy millstones, sack tackle and fly-ball governors – lethal when spinning – are packed into tight spaces. At the top beneath the curved roof are the grain bins. Grain was hauled up here in sacks and then descended again as sifting and milling machinery ground it into flour.

It is not known who built Saxtead Mill or the miller's house, dated 1810, nearby. Millwrights worked

Saxtead Green Post Mill. EH

anonymously, often in out-of-the-way places and rarely bothered with plans and drawings. Rules by which sails were made long, broad and shapely were passed on from one millwright to another. Everything was hand-made, every part of a mill as beautifully balanced as a sailing ship. Windmill language was curiously nautical too; sails were 'luffed' into the wind and millers often called stormy weather 'choppy'. When a wind blew, the whole mill creaked and swayed into life. Ropes slapped, trapdoors banged, milling gear ground away in the explosive dust; white sails turned against a blue and gold landscape.

61

Stretham Old Engine, Cambridgeshire
1831

TL 517729. 1 mile (1.6 km) S of Stretham at end of lane off A1123 [A]

Draining the Fens has occupied man for centuries. Continuous pumping and water control are essential. In the 17th and 18th centuries wooden wind-pumps were used. In the 19th century steam-powered pumping stations were introduced. By the end of the century there were over 100 working in the Fens. Stretham Old Engine is the best surviving example.

In 1813 James Smeaton suggested using a steam engine to drain the area of fen called Waterbeach Level, but it was not until 1831 that a large, single-cylinder beam engine was installed in purpose-made buildings at Stretham beside the Old West River. Forlorn-looking but full of interest, the station consists of an engine house, with attached scoopwheel and tall chimney, walled coal yard, and separate superintendent's house. A tumbledown stoker's cottage is squeezed against the scoopwheel shed. The buildings are of white brick, very plain and austere, like Fenland farm buildings. The front of the engine house, with its tall round-arched window, stone plaque and unadorned pediment, recalls early Nonconformist chapels of the region.

The inside is Piranesian. In the boiler house are three black Lancashire iron boilers. These replaced two original boilers in the 1870s. The three-storey engine house contains the giant fly-wheel, piston and drive gear and at the top the great cast-iron rocking beam. Climbing up through the building is an exhilarating experience. Stairs are stone, with simple iron hand rails. Each floor is cut away to make room for the machinery. There are dizzy openings, pits and changes of level, stairways and iron beams, and sudden sunlit glimpses of flat fields.

Until replaced by diesel and then by electric plant, Stretham Engine pumped regularly for over 100 years. It worked in a straightforward way. The coal-fired boilers produced steam which powered the beam engine which turned the large wooden scoopwheel. The scoops lifted water, 30 tons (30.48 tonnes) every turn, out of the channel which drained the fields, and into the Old West River. It was a pattern of activity which repeated itself over and over again in this disquieting, watery landscape.

Stretham Old Engine. NC

62

Waxham Great Barn, Norfolk
16th century

TG 439262. 1 mile (1.6 km) SE of
Sea Palling on B1159 coast road, 21
miles (33.7 km) N of Great
Yarmouth

[B]

The great storm of 16 October 1987
wrought terrific destruction across East
Anglia. Historic gardens, parish
churches and barns bore the brunt of
the devastation. At Waxham, on the
remote north-east coast of Norfolk, it
ripped off part of the roof of the finest
ancient barn in the county. This huge
building, over 176 ft (53.6 m) in length,
has a stupendous roof structure of tie
beams alternating with hammerbeams.
The original carpenters' construction
marks on the timbers helped to reinstate
it after the storm.

The barn was built as part of the
manor house complex of Waxham Hall,
probably by Sir Thomas Woodhouse,
High Sheriff of Norfolk, who died in
1571 and lies buried in the adjoining
church of St John. Waxham Hall appears
as a fortified house on the 1587 plan of
coastal defences which was drawn up in

the face of the Armada threat. One wing
of the house still stands, disguised by
later alterations, with its perimeter wall
and two gatehouses.

The Woodhouses had profited
handsomely at the Dissolution of the
Monasteries, acquiring a number of
properties including the celebrated
Cluniac Broomholm Priory. Not only did
this enable them to build on a grand
scale, but it may explain one unusual
feature of the barn. The big stone-
dressed buttresses, which as a rule are
found only on medieval monastic barns,
were probably re-used from one of the
priory buildings. Local materials are put
to exceptionally fine use. Norfolk Reed
covers the massive roof, of twenty
trusses with three levels of purlins. The
walls are of neatly coursed flint with
brick ventilation loops and smart red
brick diaperwork to the flank facing the
Hall. Wide cart entrances piercing this
wall and the low ranges forming yards to
each side were added in the late 18th or
early 19th century.

Only two other examples of such a
building are known in Norfolk. These
comparable, but slightly smaller, barns
are roughly contemporary and were
probably the work of the same builder.
They are at Paston, built by the famous
letter writing family, and at Godwick,

the old seat of the Cokes of Holkham. A
fourth barn of similar size survives at
the Hobart family's Hales Hall (N). In
every case the grand mansion has
disappeared or left a mere fragment as a
farmhouse, but the huge barns outlasted
their age and are only now facing crisis.

63

Wimpole Home Farm, Cambridgeshire
1794–6

TL 336510. 6 miles (9.6 km) N of
Royston off A603

[A] NT

Model farms were places where wealthy
landowners could indulge an interest in
agriculture. From the 1740s pattern
books offering examples and guidance
appeared in increasing numbers. The
ferme ornée became part of the Cult of
the Picturesque; 'primitive' farm
buildings reflected a love of Nature and
awareness of the nobility of 'the savage'.
With this in mind Philip Yorke, owner of
Wimpole Hall, commissioned John
Soane to design a farm for him. Soane
produced the Home Farm, a group of
faultless buildings which had little to do
with the real world of tottering
farmsteads and mud hovels, but still
managed a clever vernacular 'feel'.

The farm has been altered since it
was built in 1794–6 and it is not clear
how much of what survives is pure
Soane. But enough remains to provide a
good idea of what the rural reveries
performed by an intensely original
architect meant in the 1790s. Soane and
Yorke were both fascinated by
traditional building materials and
methods; they designed a mud cottage
together (although this has vanished)
and the importance of the Wimpole farm
buildings is that they wear country
dress. They were built mainly of local
timber which looked 'right' and cost less
than stone.

The Great Barn is the only surviving
timber barn designed by a leading 18th-
century English architect.
Weatherboarded and originally slate
roofed, the barn has two symmetrical

Waxham Great Barn. NCC

orches. It was used for winter
threshing and for storing corn, straw
and fodder. The Stock Sheds opposite
have tarred weatherboarding. The Cart
shed, open at the front with brick
columns and space for ten carts and
waggons, had a granary above. Behind
the Great Barn lies an intriguing dog-leg
building built from yellow bricks, with a
slate roof and a row of plank doors with
lattice grills above. Plain and forbidding,
these 'cells' were stag pens for isolating
diseased deer.

A dairy, a dovecote and a poultry
were also designed for Wimpole but do
not seem to have been built. Soane's
piggery has been demolished. The
present Dairy and Farmhouse were built
in the 1860s and reflect Victorian
farming practice and the impact of the
Gothic Revival: the Dairy resembles a
medieval chapter house.

Wimpole Home Farm goes beyond
the mere fascination with 'primitive'
materials and buildings. It was partly a
polite game and partly something else: a
deep longing for a lost Arcadia, for the
innocent beginnings of man and
agriculture; for Adam's house in
Paradise.

54
Woodbridge Tide-Mill, Suffolk
1793

TM 275487. On Tidemill Quay,
Woodbridge

A]

Watermills are an older type of building
than windmills; less spectacular and
more common. Most East Anglian rivers
had several and along the coast in one or
two places stand tide-mills, which were
always rare in England.

Woodbridge tide-mill was built in
1793 and worked until 1957. For a long
time it was clad with corrugated iron
and looked forlorn and romantic. Now
restored, it forms a focal point on the
quayside of this friendly town, its white
paintwork sparkling above the water and
mudflats of the Deben Estuary (S).
Pantiles, weatherboarding, irregularly

Woodbridge Tide Mill. NC

placed windows, a boldly projecting
'lucam'; here is the unselfconscious
charm which characterises East Anglian
mills of all kinds.

As a source of power the tide was
utterly reliable. It came in and was
impounded in a pond behind the mill
before it began to ebb. When the
impounded water was released it turned
the large water-wheel inside the mill.
The wheel is geared to the milling
equipment and plays the same part here
as sails do on a windmill. The original
millpond is now a marina, but the mill
still works with a smaller one.

Inside, almost everything is of wood
– ladders, bins, floorboards, floor

supports, cogs, shafts. There are five
floors, two of them in the mansard roof.
At the top was the lucam with its sack
hoist. Sacks were hauled up here and
grain emptied into bins. When the bins
were full, grain was released and
funnelled down through the floors for
grinding into flour. There is more room
on these floors than in a windmill, but
not much more. Hauling heavy sacks
through dusty, confined spaces with
machinery thumping away and salt
water rising beneath the floorboards was
hard work. Milling took place every
twenty-four hours; the miller led a
strange life, rising and working with the
tide and the waxing and waning moon.

7

Transport and Business

Transport and business means fetching, carrying and travelling; buying, selling and servicing. Successive modes of transport have left remains that are generally accessible today, unlike business premises which are often still in use. Eastern England's earliest transport routes were roads; prehistoric tracks like the Icknield Way which began on Salisbury Plain and ended at The Wash. They were used as drove roads and from them sprung branches and pathways which are now lost. The Roman occupation led to a network of roads linking towns and garrisons, or passing through the region on their way north. Many radiated out of London. Ermine Street, Watling Street, Stane Street, Peddars Way and Via Devana can all be traced on maps, and long sections of their routes are still followed today. The Saxons created lanes which were local and winding – there is a maze of these on the Hertfordshire–Essex border. In the Middle Ages 'pilgrim ways' developed, leading out from London and the south-east to Ely (C), Bury St Edmunds (S) and Walsingham (N). Stone bridges were thrown across rivers: there is one at Huntingdon (C) and a rare example at St Ives (C) with a chantry chapel upon it. By the end of the Middle Ages most market towns and villages were linked to one another by at least one road.

In the 17th century cattle, sheep and geese were herded by road to London's markets. Passenger-carrying stage coaches were introduced. Responsibility for keeping the 'King's Highway' in good repair fell on local parishes; in Hertfordshire and Cambridgeshire, where traffic to and from London was intense, the burden was enormous. To ease the situation, turnpikes were invented. These were roads, or parts of roads, where users paid a toll for maintenance. The first one was set up at Wadesmill (H) in 1663, on the Old North Road. The turnpike system became widespread in the 18th century.

Milestones (not seen since Roman times) were reintroduced. The Trinity Hall series between Barkway (H) and Cambridge (93, C), decorated with the college arms, are very early examples. The one at Trumpington (C) dates from 1727. A larger, finely detailed milestone stands on Alconbury Hill (C) at the junction of the Old and Great North Roads. Long-distance travel began to be glamorous. Mail coaches began to run, and coaching inns flourished. The **Scole Inn** (70, N) is a rare survivor from the pre-turnpike era.

Water transport was important from the earliest times. Until the railway age it was the only means of carrying heavy goods. Along the coast and down the eastern rivers, boats and barges plied to local fairs and markets and carried corn and wool to London. The Great Ouse linked Bedford (B) with Huntingdon, St Ives, Ely, Cambridge (via the River Cam) and King's Lynn (94, N). The River Nene linked Peterborough (C) and Wisbech (102, C). Rivers like the Stour, Chelmer, Blyth and Yare linked small market towns with the coast. The Lea was the first river in England granted an Act of Parliament (1424) for its 'improvement' as a river navigation. The 17th-century draining of the Fens opened drainage channels as through routes and, in the 18th century, old river navigations were modernised with locks, weirs and bypasses, and a handful of canals were constructed. Constable's paintings of working days on the River Stour were made at the same time as the Grand Junction Canal (now Grand Union Canal) was being cut through the Hertfordshire countryside. The Wisbech Canal relied on the tidal River Nene for water. The North Walsham and Dilham Canal (N) carried corn, flour and cabbages. Neither canal proved profitable. Most eastern waterways had become redundant before 1900, but on the Fens and Broads lighters and red-sailed wherries traded far into the 20th century.

High Lighthouse, Harwich, in 1834. RCHME

The bridge and chapel at St Ives. AFK

At ports like Wisbech, King's Lynn, Norwich (97, N) and Ipswich (S) transhipment wharves with warehouses, sheds and grain stores were built. In Wisbech the Nene is still lined with 18th- and 19th-century warehouses and King's Lynn has an important group dating from the Middle Ages onwards. Maltings, granaries and mills were built close to rivers for easy handling and despatch of goods. The great mill at Heybridge Basin (E), on the Chelmer and Blackwater Navigation, is a fine example. In smaller river towns like Mistley (E), Stowmarket (S) and St Ives there are other examples of this direct link between industry, business and transport. New docks were built at Ipswich, Lowestoft (S) and Harwich (E) in the 19th century, and these were served by railways as well as by sea-going ships.

The London and Birmingham Railway passed through Hertfordshire and Bedfordshire in the late 1830s, and railways were built throughout the region from the 1840s onwards. The terrain was easy and apart from a handful of viaducts, amongst which Digswell (H) is the largest, few major engineering works were needed. Main lines were quickly established by a group of small companies which became the Great Eastern Railway in 1862. By 1900, maps of East Anglia were covered by the GER's magenta-coloured lines. Besides these there was a wonderful collection of 'goods only', seaside and farmers' lines. the 'Gin and Toffee' line ran from Elsenham (E) to Thaxted (E); the 'Sugar Track' from Bishop's Stortford (H) to Braintree (E); and 'Crab and Winkle' from Kelvedon (E) to Tollesbury Pier (E), carrying jam, crabs, winkles and oysters. Newmarket had a gorgeous terminus but its line suffered terrible financial problems, as did the Mid-Suffolk Light Railway. The Colchester, Stour Valley, Sudbury and Halstead Railway Company built a huge viaduct at **Chappel** (68, E) which is still in use.

There was rich variety in railway architecture. In the 1840s Needham Market (S), Stowmarket and Bury St Edmunds were graced with Jacobean style stations. Francis Thompson designed plain, but good-looking buildings at Cambridge, Great Chesterford (E) and Audley End (E). Norwich is in a Free Renaissance style, Letchworth (H) has an Arts and Crafts flavour. Village stations were often delightful; in Bedfordshire a series of homely cottage *orné* stations were built along the Bedford to Bletchley line (**Bedford Railway**, 66, B). After the Second World War nationalisation drastically reduced the railways. One or two country routes like the Cromer (N) branch remain, but the independent lines, under-funded and always sweet and slow, have gone.

Development of transport goes hand-in-hand with the growth of towns and business. By the Middle Ages a network of market towns had developed in eastern England. King's Lynn and Wisbech have market places which were deliberately planned and spacious; Norwich once had separate hay, madder and cattle markets, and was an important business centre from Saxon times onwards. St Ives had a famous wool market. There are medieval shops in Lavenham (95, S) and Saffron Walden (E), where narrow streets like Butcher Row, Fish Row and Mercer Row were once lines of temporary stalls. The **Ancient House, Ipswich** (65, S) is a fine example of a prosperous merchant's house. It dates from the 15th to the 17th century, by which time the East Anglian cloth trade was in its long-drawn decline, and the region was becoming something of a backwater. The Industrial Revolution made little initial impact on eastern England but there were advances in agriculture, and the corn and malting trade continued to be important. There are good corn exchanges at Sudbury (S), Saffron Walden and at Bury St Edmunds.

From the 18th century shops began developing into their modern form, often with symmetrical fronts and large

The Corn Exchange, Bury St Edmunds. AFK

windows: Bury St Edmunds has some interesting examples. Shopping arcades appeared in the 19th century, although not many were built; the Art Nouveau Royal Arcade at Norwich is the best. Specialised business premises took the form of private and joint stock banks and insurance offices, often carried out in mixed revival styles, like Lloyds Bank in Cambridge, and Barclays at Bank Plain, Norwich. Architecturally, the most confident and ebullient-looking business premises are Edwardian, amongst which Skipper's original Norwich Union Offices, Norwich is supreme.

The modern world has contributed its own functional aesthetic to the region: the M1, M11, M25 motorways; electrified railways; Felixstowe Container Port (E); Cambridge Science Park (C); business parks and offices of all kinds; out-of-town supermarkets with acres of car parking. **Cardington Airship Hangars** (67, B) are heroic structures, and **Stansted Airport** (71, E) and the **Willis Corroon Building** (73, S) are examples of excellent 20th-century design.

65

Ancient House, Ipswich, Suffolk
15th–19th century

TM 164444. Buttermarket, Ipswich town centre

[C]

'More ornate and gayer than any other house of its date in England' was how Pevsner described the Ancient House. Better known as Sparrowe's House, after the family which owned it for 300 years, the building (which is now a workshop) gave its distinctive oriel windows to the Arts and Crafts style. The grand street frontage with its breathtaking display of pargeting is a lavish and robust celebration of the Restoration, centred around the huge Royal Arms of Charles II. A great projecting shelf of a cornice protects the plaster moulded in high relief, with abundant swags representing the Elements Earth, Air and Water. Beneath the windows are the continents

The Ancient House, Ipswich. JB

of Europe, Asia, America and Africa – no Australia, for it had, of course, yet to be discovered. A riot of decoration includes mythological creatures, a charming bucolic scene, Atlas bearing the globe and St George and the Dragon. The vigorous oak carving on the ground floor was restored in the 19th century.

In the late 15th century when Sir Thomas Fastolf, MP acquired part of the bustling fishmarket in the commercial heart of the town to build his new house, the port of Ipswich was prospering from the cloth trade. But, unlike less broad-based towns such as Lavenham (95, S), which were wholly dependent on that trade, Ipswich was still flourishing in the 17th century. The Ancient House evolved as a home and place of business for a long succession of well-to-do fishmongers, drapers and grocers, like William Sparrowe. He successfully campaigned to have the malodorous market relocated soon after buying the house for £400 in c.1600. It was his great grandson, Robert (d.1698), who added the swanky front range c.1660.

Like many townhouses, the Ancient House has a complex history of multiple phases of building, exploiting to the full the cramped urban site. Its wealthy owners combined an eye for fashion with a healthy respect for the quality works of

their predecessors, which has left a remarkable sequence of interior decoration demonstrating the growing standards of comfort and changes in taste from the 15th to the 18th century. In the late 16th century the courtyard was enclosed with a glazed long gallery. Medieval crenellated timber beams gave way to plaster ceilings and Renaissance wall-paintings to rare painted hangings and oak panelling to counter the draughts. Finally, on the ground floor, the gorgeously weighty early plasterwork gives way to mid-18th century light and decorative rococo.

66

Bedford Railway, Bedfordshire
1846

TL 041498 and SP 869337. Bedford to Bletchley

[C]

Deepest, remotest Bedfordshire by train. In the 1950s C S Lewis often travelled this line on his way from Oxford to Cambridge. Services were old-fashioned, infrequent and slow. Lewis dubbed his train the 'Cantab. Crawler'. The middle

Ridgmont Station. BCC

part of his journey was spent on what began as the Bedford Railway, which ran between Bedford and Bletchley in Buckinghamshire. It opened in 1846 and was absorbed almost immediately into the LNWR. There were grand ideas for this line; it was going to link East Anglian ports with South Wales. It never did. Part of it is single track. Manned level crossings still have white wooden gates with big red circles in the middle; gate lamps are lit by hand each night. This is a working line full of character and detail.

Late afternoon trains are best. Leaving Buckinghamshire at Fenny Stratford – the first station after Bletchley, with cottage, trees and signal-box – the line winds unhurriedly out into Bedfordshire. Straggling edges of villages give way to cornfields. Semaphore signals are silhouetted against the sky; red and white, or yellow and black for 'distant' signals, with a V cut out of them. Ancient diesels dawdle across points and level crossings; rusting wagons and empty sidings are overgrown with blackberry and willow-herb.

The countryside is homely and yet strange. Strange too are the village stations along the way. Fenny Stratford, Woburn Sands (both in Buckinghamshire), Ridgmont (B) and Millbrook (B) are in

the 'Old English Cottage' style popular in the 1830s. Half-timbered, with gables, dormers, bargeboards and other trimmings; designed as picturesque additions to the Duke of Bedford's estates. Their cosy look reassured the traveller of 1846, for beyond the cottage door and waiting-room fire was a newly invented world of iron and steam.

Aspley Guise (B), Stewartby (100, B) and Kempston Hardwick (B) still have wooden platforms, and there are wooden waiting shelters with frilly valancing, crossing-keepers' huts with vertical boarding, and buff-painted signal boxes. Millbrook has a low, brick-paved, stone-edged platform. This is the heart of the working brickfields and the train rumbles right through the middle. Tall chimneys soar skywards on either side; there are huge stacks of pink bricks, gaping kilns, dusty yards and loaded freight wagons shunted into sidings. Black stripes on white squares indicate crossings of the line. The brickyards peter out into a landscape of water-filled pits, fields and ash trees. The train finally sneaks into Bedford through a scrappy mixture of empty railway land, allotments and a chocolate factory. There is a glimpse of the river, an elegant bridge, rowing boats – then the end of the line. It is no longer possible to journey on as C S Lewis did to

Cambridge, all services having been withdrawn on 1 January 1968.

67

Cardington Airship Hangars, Bedfordshire
1916–27

TL 081469. 3 miles (4.8 km) SE of Bedford off A600

[D]

Two giant sheds lend scale and drama to a flat countryside. These steel envelopes belong to the same functional tradition as the great boat stores at Royal Dockyards, and were built to hangar airships at Short Brothers' Naval Aircraft Works.

The Germans pioneered rigid airship construction; the first Zeppelin flew in 1900. By the end of the First World War nine British airship stations had been built, the last one being Cardington. The great No 1 Shed was put up in 1916–17 and enlarged in 1926–27. No 2 Shed was built later in the 1920s. Each shed covers 4½ acres (1.8 ha). Each has a wide central nave and double side aisles. Walls and roofs are plainly clad in corrugated steel sheeting and there are huge sliding doors at the west end of each shed, powered by electric motors. Originally there was a large mooring mast, a gasworks, and fitting shops nearby. These have gone, but a sombre administration block and a model village for the works staff remain.

In the 1920s and 1930s British governments took rigid airships seriously. Cigar-shaped, cumbersome, and ultimately tragic, many were built at

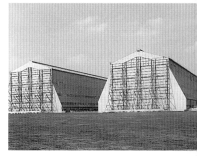

Cardington airship hangars. RCHME

Cardington. The designs were all very similar: a long, lightweight wood or metal framework braced with wires, stuffed with gas-filled balloons, and covered with a skin of specially treated fabric. Slung underneath were engine cars and passenger cabins, quaintly called 'gondolas'. The main drawback with these airships was that they were pumped full of hydrogen.

The biggest airship built at Cardington in the 1920s was R101. Hastily designed and ill-conceived, it was hangared in No 1 Shed. In October 1930, R101 set off on a much publicised long-distance flight to India. Over Beauvais in France it went out of control and struck the ground. Five-and-a-half million cubic feet of hydrogen exploded, killing most of those on board. It was the end of big British airships.

Cardington's giant sheds are awesome from close at hand. From far away, along the hilltop road to Old Warden they slant upwards out of yellow and pea-coloured fields. And in their unreal still-life forms are archetypal echoes: ancient temples, pyramids, cathedrals, ocean liners, and the great Crystal Palace.

68

Chappel Viaduct, Essex
1849

TL 897285. Crosses A604 at Chappel, 7½ miles (12 km) W of Colchester

[C]

'Railway mania' gave birth to many exotic and resoundingly named companies. One was the Colchester, Stour Valley, Sudbury and Halstead Railway. The grand aim of this company was to build a line from Marks Tey (E) to Sudbury (S), with a branch to Halstead (E) thrown in. In 1849 all of its 19 miles (30.5 km) were opened to traffic. Later the line was extended to Cambridge (C). For a country railway stringing together a handful of market towns it was splendidly appointed; there were large stations in remote villages, and painted signal-boxes in the middle of nowhere. At Chappel, a spectacular viaduct carried

Chappel Viaduct. DP

the line across the valley of the River Colne.

The viaduct was designed by a local man, Peter Bruff; it is 355 yds (324.6 m) long, with 32 arches, and it used up 7,000,000 locally made bricks. Fitness for purpose and a bold relationship between form and materials – which typify the best achievements of the railway age – are much in evidence here. It may lack the ruthless scale of Digswell Viaduct (H) but its simple geometry remains uncluttered by overhead wires and can be the better appreciated.

Contemporaries found the scale of new railway structures startling, and they were painted quite early on by artists who saw in them strong elements of the Picturesque and Sublime. Time has absorbed England's railway viaducts into the landscape but often, as here, they remain the central part of a rural scene.

There are different views of Chappel Viaduct from the narrow roads and footpaths which wind in and out of the village. On a still day, with its deep arches thrown into relief by sunlight and shadow, the viaduct has an unsought-for grandeur. From underneath, the view along the arches cut through the piers is like an endless, pillared hall.

Chappel Viaduct was made wide enough to take double tracks, although it never got them. The expected passenger expresses never appeared. Occasionally a Seaside Special came shouting through the quiet fields and villages of Suffolk: unglamorous mixed-goods trains were more common. In the 1960s the lines to Cambridge and to Halstead closed. The original 1849 line is now a sleepy branch known to local commuters as 'The Slug'.

At Chappel Station there is a railway museum and the best way to get there is by slow train (there are no fast ones anyway). From the curved siding at Marks Tey old diesels amble towards Sudbury. Blue smoke lingers in the air; signals clunk up and down; hawthorn and elder close in upon the tracks, and there is one glorious moment as the train fusses its way across Chappel Viaduct.

69

High and Low Lighthouses, Harwich, Essex
1817–18

TM 263324. Harwich, 15 miles (24 km) E of Colchester on A120. In West Street

[C]

Harwich was founded in the 12th century by the Bigod Earls of Norfolk and the port flourished as the shortest sea crossing to the Low Countries. As early as the 17th century mariners had been guided by twin beacons set up above the town gate and on the shore as leading lights which, when lined up, indicated the harbour channel. For 150 years a sea-coal fire and candle lantern had to be kept burning, but in 1817 John Rennie drew up plans on behalf of Trinity House for a pair of new lighthouses on the same site, equipped with the newly invented Argand lamps and reflectors.

Asher Alexander, Surveyor to Trinity House, designed an elegant pair of polygonal towers in fashionable gault brick. The Low Light, now a museum, has been somewhat disguised by a coat of paint and the addition of a beachfront shelter. The High Light was originally something of a misnomer, since the light itself was, on the advice of local 'experts', sited at its former level about half-way up the 70 ft (21.3 m) tower. Predictably, this was soon found to be a mistake and the light was moved to its present position. The projecting original canopy stranded at half-mast and the polygonal cap give the building a mildly exotic feel, with a hint of the pagoda. In true Regency spirit, this graceful but functional building with its trim, nautical form becomes an eyecatcher and a delightful incident in the townscape.

Smartly detailed throughout, the windows and doors are finished in milled stone. A flight of stone steps with bowed iron railings gives access to the first floor, below which is a vaulted storage basement. Inside, all is neat and shipshape. The timber stair winds up past partitioned rooms each with a fireplace and cupboard beneath the stairs. No machinery survives in the lantern chamber, but the climb is worth the effort for the panoramic view of the bay.

The Lights became obsolete as early as the 1840s after massive extraction of septaria for the manufacture of Roman cement changed the course of the harbour channel. In the earlier part of this century, the High Light acquired a new significance to sailors as home to one 'Lighthouse Lil'. Today, it is to become a television and wireless museum.

70

Scole Inn, Scole, Norfolk
1655

TM 149789. On A140 at Scole, 24 miles (38.6 km) N of Ipswich
[C]

The White Hart, now the Scole Inn, was purpose built as a coaching inn on the main road from London to Norwich via Ipswich, by the wealthy Norwich merchant John Peck, who placed his Arms and the date 1655 on the central gable. It was distinguished by a great timber sign spanning the road, which alone cost the staggering sum of £1,057. Sumptuously carved with allegorical, biblical and hunting scenes, it was described by a contemporary as 'the noblest sighne post in England'. By 1801 however, it was looked upon as 'a pompous sign, with ridiculous ornaments' and was soon taken down. It is known from an early 19th-century print which also shows that a pair of canted bays and two porches have been

The Scole Inn. JB

removed. The tripartite sashes replace mullion and transom windows.

This robust exercise in Artisan Mannerist mode, characterised by the Dutch gables, giant rusticated pilasters, heavy cornice and tall panelled stacks, is a vigorous celebration of red brickwork. The style is that of the craftsman builders, strongly influenced by Netherlands Renaissance architecture. The classic Norfolk example of the type is Raynham Hall, *c*.1635 (not open to the public). Norfolk has a large number of fine brick houses of the later 16th to 17th century with crow-stepped or curved gables showing Flemish influence. The earlier ones often combined brick and timber like the Scole Inn where the timber rear wall to the courtyard is finished in rusticated plaster to mimic stone.

Inside, the lofty public rooms have inglenook fireplaces and chunky woodwork. The great staircase with its massive turned balusters, square newel posts carved with lozenges and ovals surmounted by urn finials and dog gates impresses by its gusto rather than finesse. The Inn once boasted a prodigious circular bed, reputed to

house 30–40 persons, surpassed only by the famous Bed of Ware.

71

Stansted Airport, Essex
1991

Off junction 8 of the M11, 1½ miles (2.4 km) E on A120
[C]

There is a new spirit at Stansted Airport that brings back the exhilaration of travel. The architects, Foster Associates, have achieved a boldness, clarity and order which is instructive when set against the chaotic experience of most other airports. Gatwick tried to be like this and failed. The vision behind Stansted was simple: road – shed – aircraft – runway – take off!

The approaches to Stansted are straightforward, landscaping is unfussy. From the car park, the terminal looks like a temple on a plinth. Against the rising whine of unseen jet engines a 'processional' way leads towards the plinth through glass doors and across a flying walkway. Ritual and drama combine. Immediately below is the railway station, an open-ended concrete cutting with steel-shod columns, a coffered ceiling and friendly lighting. Green and silver trains wait. Ramps, walkways, escalators, lead up, down and across. This is exciting. Walk around – enjoy different views, change levels, explore space – without ever feeling lost. Glazed ramps rise beneath the great *porte cochère* and join the main concourse inside the terminal.

First impressions of the concourse are of space and structure; of architecture and engineering blended together. Polished granite floors are austerely smart. Lightness falls from the suffused geometry of the roof, which is supported by tubular steel 'trees'. These disciplined forms are as clear about their function as the struts and wings on an aeroplane. They carry neat black pods containing services, signs, and other equipment. The eye is led along their crisp lines, away to the edges of the building and the tinted, gas-filled, double-glazed curtain walls.

Stansted is smaller than many international airports. The original concept that everything should be on one level and refreshingly 'open' has been modified by operational requirements. But travellers entering the terminal and moving smoothly towards their aircraft are still taking part in an exciting human drama. Orientation is clear, colours are not strident, symbols are easily understood. The final link with the aircraft is via a satellite building reached by a transit shuttle. More satellites can be added as needed. Baggage-handling and essential services are out of sight in the terminal's undercroft.

Twilight is the best time to visit Stansted. The terminal glows like 1001 Nights. Lights wink, glimmer, and roar past. Images come to mind: 1930s gliding clubs, the crunchy style of Imperial Airways, travel in aeroplanes, flight. Suddenly the architecture of this

Stansted Airport, entrance forecourt. KK/FA

place touches the heart, and is undeniably beautiful.

72

Stocker's Lock, Grand Union Canal, Hertfordshire
18th–20th century

TQ 052935. 1 mile (1.6 km) S of Rickmansworth. Reached by a footpath off Harefield Road
[C]

The Grand Union Canal is the longest and once the busiest inland waterway in England. It runs from London to Birmingham: 136 miles (218.8 km), through 166 locks. The Grand Union was a 1929 grouping of several older canals; a last-ditch attempt to take waterborne trade into the 20th century. The part which runs from the Thames at Brentford in London to Braunston in Northamptonshire, was originally the Grand Junction. It was engineered by William Jessop, and constructed with huge effort and haste, mainly between 1793 and 1800. It proved to be one of the saner episodes of canal mania.

Jessop's canal belongs to England's 'heroic' period of waterways: fairly straight lines; valleys crossed on big embankments; a massive cutting at Tring (H); locks wide enough to take 70 ton (71.1 tonne) barges. One of those locks is number 82, named Stocker's after a long-serving lock-keeper.

From a distance Stocker's is the silhouette of a house, the curving lines of a bridge, the straight angles of balance beams and the flicker of moving water. Close-up it is brick and stone, black and white paint, cast-iron paddle gearing, and sudden changes of level. Balance beams are lined and wrinkled, brickwork pock-marked and scuffed; everything here has been used, repaired, renewed, repainted and used again.

The lock-keeper's cottage is low at the front and tall at the back because of its sloping site; a shaping by need that is typical of canals, where everything has a purpose. The large house was built for a coal clerk who collected dues from passing boats. Just below the lock, on the towpath, stands a London Coal Dues boundary marker. In its heyday the canal was profitable and traffic was heavy. Loads of coal, timber, stone,

bricks, corn, copper, and later iron, steel, cheese, cement, paper and limejuice, were carried by day and night. Cargoes were local as well as long-distance. Big barges were a tight fit in Grand Junction locks but narrow-boats went through two at a time. They had names like Alice, Kate and Madge, and cabins painted with roses, castles and numbers; a homely mix of fantasy and function echoed in the strangely shaped paddle gearing which lets water in and out of Stocker's Lock.

73

Willis Corroon Building, Suffolk
1973–5

TM 162444. Friars Street, Ipswich
[D]

This is the sexiest building in East Anglia. A dusky, seamless glass wall, full of caressing reflections; cool and sensuous by day, warm and glowing by night. Formerly the Willis Faber building, it was designed by Norman Foster for a family firm of insurance brokers who wanted to expand their offices, and was built in 1973–5. It lies on the edge of a commercial zone between the old market centre of Ipswich and the railway.

The size and shape of this building are ambiguous; the childish urge to walk round and round and then press one's nose against the glass is irresistible. For, with sleek irony, this modern office forever reflects the older buildings nearby, especially the Unitarian Meeting House (46, S) which is right next door. A 20th-century place of work; a 17th-century place of worship: the relationship between them is a real visual treat.

The Willis Corroon building is constructed as a frame of concrete columns supporting waffle slab floors. The reflective curtain of tinted and toughened glass hangs from rooftop level. The spacious, uncluttered interior, open-plan on two floors, and centred around a cascade of open escalators, demonstrated a fresh approach in the

Stocker's Lock. DP

Willis Corroon building by night. RCHME

mid-1970s. It provided working conditions of a high standard, and excellent staff facilities – restaurant, rooftop garden, gymnasium, swimming pool – were designed to share the same building as desks and filing cabinets. All this was done partly to attract staff away from London and partly to help with local recruitment, but it broke new ground by reversing engrained British concepts about 'work' and 'play', and the traditional separation of these important activities.

Willis Corroon expresses ideas about space, internal visibility, lighting, movement and detail, which are brilliantly up-dated at Stansted Airport (71, E) – there the romance of flight, here the glamour of work – both magic-making places which can never be repeated.

8

Country Houses

Eastern England is rich in country houses, although some periods and styles are better represented than others. There is little stone, and brick was important early on. Over half of England's brick buildings from before 1550 occur in the region. Wealthy private men wanted fashionable houses, and brick lent itself to the impulse to display, the aimed-for grand scale that was vital to the period of late medieval building. There are big brick angle towers at Faulkborne Hall (E) (after 1429) and a flickering, moulded brick and terracotta skyline at East Barsham (N) – best of a lavish group of houses of the 1520s. Proudest of all is **Layer Marney Towers** (83, E) which mingles Renaissance with traditional Gothic motifs.

The late 16th to early 17th century was as great a period of country house building as it was of literature. Splendid houses were built to entertain kings and queens. At the same time new Renaissance ideas were being absorbed, some slowly, others quickly and weirdly. The planning of many houses was still medieval and inward-looking – courtyards, halls, residual gate-towers – but others were H- or E-plan and their appearance was being transformed. Avant-garde houses like **Burghley** (77, C), **Hatfield** (78, C), **Blickling** (76, N), **Audley End** (75, E) (and others now vanished), were a glittering effervescence of heraldry, turrets, columns, strapwork and buccaneering angles. These buildings are known as 'prodigy houses' on account of their size and lavishness. They belong to an age whose contrasts were perfectly expressed in its architecture.

More modest houses like **Houghton House** (81, B) lead on to the Artisan Mannerism type of gentry houses characterised by good quality brickwork and a Dutch-inspired use of classical features and shapely gables. Tyttenhanger (H) is an example; Raynham Hall (N), odd and transitional,

is another. By the mid-17th century this Mannerism was overlapping with an insular classicism of the type displayed in **Wimpole Hall** (84, C), Thorpe Hall (C) and Melton Constable (N), a style perhaps inspired by the Prince's Lodging at Newmarket (S), a disappeared building by the courtier Inigo Jones. This English classicism flourished after the Restoration, its plain walls, regular windows and hipped roofs drifting happily into what is usually meant by 'Georgian'.

At the end of the 17th century baroque flowered briefly in the region only to be hustled away leaving Archer's gorgeous Wrest Park Pavilion (90, B), the interior of Burghley and little else. Baroque did not catch on in 18th-century England. Instead, the English love affair with Italy – succoured by a hundred years or so of Grand Touring – began to harden into purer statements of classical style and learning. It became a 'movement' with leaders, followers and heroes. The heroes were Andrea Palladio and Inigo Jones. The leaders were Burlington, Kent, Campbell. The architecture, called Palladian, was very English; based on learned architectural books, the sights of the Grand Tour, politics and the 'Rule of Taste'. Again, the eastern counties led the way. Campbell's (now demolished) Wanstead (E) of c.1715 and his **Houghton Hall** (80, N) created national precedents. A main block with a grand portico linked to lower outlying wings, set in the hushed beauty of a landscaped park, became the standard type. Kent took his cue from Campbell and designed the magisterial, austere **Holkham Hall** (79, N). In houses like this all the richness and display were kept on the inside. Wimpole Hall and Woburn (B) were remodelled, Moor Park (H) was built with a huge portico, Wolterton (N) was more homespun but still followed the noble pattern, Heveningham (S) in the 1770s was late Palladian, but still on a grand scale.

Houghton Hall, the Stone Hall, AFK

Hatfield House, the south front. AFK

Towards the end of the 18th century architectural design began to lose its severity. Out of Palladianism came neo-classicism and 'taste' become ever more 'tasteful'. Southill (B) is the ultimate Regency 'gentleman's house'. Robert Adam – who created a dashing classical style of his own – appeared at Audley End and Kimbolton (C). Soane's strange esoteric genius left its mark at Wimpole Hall and in a handful of much smaller, sparsely detailed houses. At **Ickworth** (82, S), a startling, unfinished rotunda marks the end of the period. Like the

earlier Palladian houses it was designed as a place to display art collected in Italy. Like most of them it had a park landscaped by 'Capability' Brown.

Picturesque and 'Gothick' had appeared half-way through the 18th century but the full blast of Romantic revivals came with the 19th century. Most important was the Gothic Revival. **Ashridge** (74, H) is early and rambling, Knebworth (H) later and excruciating. Wrest Park is French, an unusual style for the 1830s. Shrubland Park (S) is 1830s Italianate. Jacobean Revival

reached its zenith in 1850 at Somerleyton (S). Royal Sandringham, begun in 1870, is a later neo-Jacobean house at the centre of the largest estate in Norfolk. Elveden (S) has a great Indian hall and was built for a maharajah. By the end of the century, baroque, Queen Anne and Georgian were all being reinterpreted with varying degrees of success.

In a swing away from the excesses of the 19th century the early 20th century was a period when country houses returned to a more traditional Arts and Crafts style, free of revival tags, but owing something to vernacular buildings of the English countryside. Big houses were built using cottage-sized materials. Lutyens, the most brilliant of the traditionalists, designed Overstrand Hall (N) and E S Prior was highly original in his use of Norfolk brick, flint and pantiles for Home Place (N). Detmar Blow built Happisburgh Manor in 1900 (N). For the rest of the 20th century, eastern England was unfashionable and country-house building, for the most part, settled back into comfortable but unadventurous neo-Georgian.

74

Ashridge Park, Hertfordshire
19th century

SP 993122. 3 miles (4.8 km) N of Berkhamsted off B4506

Gardens [A] House [D]

Castle, abbey, palace or collegiate pile? The 19th century could not decide what Ashridge was meant to be. Repton, who created the original gardens there, summed it up as 'a modern House, on a large scale, where the character of the rich Gothic of Henry VII has been successfully introduced and imitated.'

Ashridge was built in 1808–13 by James Wyatt and enlarged in 1820 by his son Sir Jeffry Wyattville. Wyatt was an early exponent of the Gothic Revival. He had looked hard at real medieval architecture and he knew how to design picturesquely. He was talented but lazy, and his building methods were slapdash. His most dramatic house, Fonthill

Knebworth House, Hertfordshire. RCHME

...shridge Park from the south. AFK

Wiltshire), had a madly sensational
...ower which collapsed a few years after
...ompletion. At Ashridge, Wyatt decided
...o go for length rather than height.

The house sprawls romantically
...cross its site, anchored by its square
...keep' and its chapel spire. The 'keep'
...which rises above a dizzy staircase hall
...as designed by Wyattville, the chapel
...y Wyatt. Each is a perfect foil to the
...ther. In 1813 the chapel was one of the
...most convincing revivalist essays so far
...uilt in England. The main entrance has
...arved heraldry and ogee-topped turrets
...hat bring to mind King's College
...Chapel (30, C). Inside there is fan-
...aulting. Piled behind and stretched out
...long either side is the spectacular
...umble of turrets, loopholes, moulded
...windows and battlements that make up
...he house. Facade gallops after facade,
...ach displaying details which often have
...Perpendicular sources. Yet, inside, the
...main rooms relate to one another in the
...usual formal classical way. The
...medievalising is only skin-deep.

Contemporaries found Ashridge
...idiculous or incongruous. Prince
...Puckler-Muskau visited in the 1820s and
...was amazed to find it looked like a
...'ortress' set in the midst of peaceful
...ields and 'pretty flower-gardens'. In
...814–20 Repton designed fifteen
...ifferent small gardens including a rock
...arden, a physic garden, a winter
...arden, a monks' garden, an arboretum,
... paved terrace, an embroidered
...arterre, and a rosary with a holy well.
...le called it a gallery of 'different styles,
...ates, characters, and dimensions.' The
...rregularity and mixture of these

gardens complemented that of the
house. Some idea of Repton's work can
still be seen in the Rosarie and the
Monks' Garden.

Set on a level site with surrounding
woodland and heath, Ashridge lies half-
way between 18th-century 'Gothick' and
full-blown Victorian Gothic. It is an
exceptional early example of a style
which became a national passion
embracing the design of everything;
from kitchen furniture and railway
stations, to dog kennels and the Houses
of Parliament.

75

Audley End House, Essex
17th–19th century

TL 525382. 1 mile (1.6 km) W of
Saffron Walden off B1383

[A] EH

This was once the largest house in
England and its appearance provided the
illusion of incalculable size. Most of it
was pulled down in the 18th century but
a proud fragment of this Jacobean
'prodigy house' remains.

Audley End was built in c.1603–16
for Thomas Howard, Earl of Suffolk,
Lord Treasurer of England. The
architect was reputedly Bernart Janssen,
who sculpted, built and decorated in an
elaborate Anglo-Flemish style. Like
Hatfield House (78, H), Audley End was
intended as a 'royal residence' and
Howard hoped that James I would make
a 'progress' there. The house followed
medieval patterns by being built around

two courtyards, with a hall occupying
the central range. The hall divided two
sets of great apartments, intended for
the king and queen who visited only
once. Two years after Audley End was
finished, Howard fell from favour, was
stripped of office and disgraced. His vast
house became a dinosaur. Half was
pulled down in 1721, the rest sold later
in a semi-derelict condition. Defoe
passed by in 1722 and saw the decaying
ruins of this 'most magnificent pile'.
Only the Hall range and its
accompanying wings survived.

The front is stone-faced and
symmetrical, with two showpiece
porches, crowded with columns and
ornate strapwork. One gives entry into
the Hall via the screens passage. Here, as
at Hatfield, the screen is a massive
two-storeyed affair, full of rude vigour
and covered all over with carved panels
and figures. At the other end of the Hall,
facing this barbarous Jacobean mêlée, is
a plain stone screen with a plain stone
staircase behind it. This is 18th-century
work and is probably by Vanbrugh. He
gave this staircase an intriguing ceiling
(which is easy to miss) just like an early
17th-century fretwork ceiling but
altogether crisper, more slender and
more sophisticated than the real thing.
It is a delightful and very early instance
of Jacobean revival.

This rich mix of dates and styles of
decoration continues throughout the
house. The Saloon has a good 17th-
century ceiling with icy pendants,
frolicking whales, mermaids and sea-
monsters. The wooden South Stairs are

Audley End House. EH

also 17th century; a less ambitious variation on the Hatfield theme. Other rooms pick up the Jacobean revival again and have ceilings tricked out with thin frets and pendants dating from the 1780s.

The 'Gothick' Chapel dates from the same period. Its fireplace, fan-vaulted gallery and dolly-mixture colours are unexpected and pretty. Robert Adam decorated a suite of rooms in the south wing: the Dining Parlour has his usual two screens of columns at either end, and the Little Drawing Room is in his enticing Etruscan style.

Adam also designed the handsome stone road bridge over the lake in the park. This was landscaped by 'Capability' Brown in the 1760s and scattered with half-hidden, half-revealed monuments and garden pieces. The horizons from the house are thick with trees. An eye-catching domed temple peeps down mysteriously from a wooded hillside to the west. East of the house on rising ground stands the Temple of Concord; a daft little building with no roof, built in 1791 to celebrate George III's recovery from madness.

76

Blickling Hall, Norfolk
17th–18th century

TG 179284. 1½ miles (2.4 km) NW of Aylsham on B1354

[A] NT

Blickling was the last of the 'prodigy houses'. Its sudden appearance set back from a bend in the Aylsham road is immensely romantic. Smooth lawns and hedges, bold profiles and a careless backdrop of trees make this a genuine piece of theatre. Its architect, Robert Lyminge, had designed Hatfield House (78, H) a few years earlier and from there no doubt came the kicked-up gables, the ogee-crowned turrets and the stone porch. But Blickling is scaled down; less bossy and more beautiful. A narrow site caused Lyminge to build two separate low wings which stand forward from the main front. They are built of the same bonfire-red bricks as the house, with strong, decorative 'Dutch' gables,

Blickling Hall, the entrance front. AFK

dated 1624. Two huge yew hedges, themselves 'live' architectural features, complete the symmetry of the forecourt.

Blickling was built in 1616–27 for Sir Henry Hobart, a wealthy Suffolk lawyer who became Lord Chief Justice. The date 1620 appears above the front entrance but, despite having kept its figure, much of the house was remodelled by the Ivory family of architects in the 1760s. To their work belong the north and west fronts, well-mannered but tame compared to the south front. Inside, the Ivorys made more alterations, creating an extraordinary staircase in what was the Great Hall. They used much of Lyminge's original woodwork for this.

Elsewhere in the house they re-sited Jacobean chimneys, overmantels, and other bits and pieces.

Like Hatfield, Blickling has a Long Gallery. To step into this room is to be swept along by a twisting, foaming white ceiling. It was the work of Edward Stanyan, and nowhere is the early 17th-century fetish for all-over decoration better expressed. Ribs, scrolls, studs, pendants are scrambled up with thirty-one panels filled with symbolism and story-telling images. A virgin sits on a dragon, a woman is pecked by an eagle, a man bitten by a dog; there is a rhinoceros (fabulous beast) and Henry Hobart's coat of arms.

At the end of this lavish Gallery a door leads into the Peter the Great Room. Take two steps, and decoration of 1630 is replaced by that of 1780: pink and peach colours; dainty and restrained plasterwork. Stand in the doorway and both ceilings can be seen at once. The contrast makes one flinch. Less of a shock is the State Bedroom, in tasteful Ionian gold and white, with a bed borrowed from George II.

The gardens at Blickling are a mixture of 18th-century relaxed and 1930s formal. Pleasing views of the house can be had from the raised terrace or by circling through the groves of mature oaks, beeches and yew. A Tuscan Temple and an Orangery date from the glory days. The gardens are not extensive but the park is. A large artificial lake, scattered trees, browsing sheep – all the favourite ingredients, plus a bizarre stone Mausoleum in the shape of a pyramid.

77

Burghley House, Cambridgeshire
16th–18th century

TF 048061. 1½ miles (2.4 km) N of A1 (T), on SE side of Stamford
[A]

Lions and unicorns, chimneys, cupolas, obelisks and mini-castles: the fantastic skyline of Burghley House captures perfectly the visual richness of Elizabethan England. This is the architecture of adventure, New Learning, and the Court of the Faerie Queen. Burghley was built by William Cecil, Elizabeth I's Chief Minister and a precise and extravagant patron of architecture. For thirty years or so he was building something, somewhere; his London house, the massive Theobalds Park for his son, Burghley House for himself and as a reception for his queen. Royal progresses were part of Elizabeth's cult of sovereignty. Each year the whole Court descended on the house of some great noble and stayed for half the summer. The entertainment was lavish, the cost fabulous. The houses built for

these occasions are rightly called 'prodigy houses'.

Cecil's house is typical of that heady confection of ideas and motifs which characterises much 16th-century architecture. Its courtyard plan and great hall are medieval in form, its gatehouse harks back to earlier Tudor work like Layer Marney Towers (83, E) or Cambridge colleges (93, C), such as Trinity, Christ's and St John's. But mixed in with these conservative

features are others which come from the enlightened Court circle of Protector Somerset, from the Italian Renaissance, France and the Netherlands.

The tall bay windows and the regular symmetry of the north front owe a debt to the great Longleat in Wiltshire. The obelisk clock tower, a mad, exotic chess-piece imprisoned in the courtyard, was inspired by French examples and by Flemish decoration. Originally the courtyard had an Italianate open

Burghley House. RCHME

colonnade, now filled in. Above, there is the glorious roof line, with its spiky parapets and Doric column-and-entablature chimneys lifted from some Continental book on the Five Orders. The mixing of supple classical motifs with coarser English and Flemish work may appear naive, but it is bursting with energy and passion. It was vital to the sought-after effects of mass and silhouette; the poetry of 'gorgeous palaces'.

Inside Burghley the same apparent confusion continues. The great hall has a medieval hammerbeam roof but a classical chimney piece. There is a tunnel-vaulted staircase coffered in the French style, but its landing has a medieval rib-vault with pendants. There is little that remains of the 16th century inside.

In the last quarter of the 17th century almost the whole interior of Burghley was redecorated in the baroque style. The important suite of state rooms was decorated by Verrio. The Heaven Room is staggering – a *trompe l'oeil* riot of half-dressed cherubs, birds, gods, goddesses, roses and naked buttocks, all framed by classical columns. Craziest of all is a horse and rider which suddenly plunge headlong from the entablature. Verrio impishly put himself in amongst the mythological figures – he is the bald man sitting in the Cyclops' forge. The Hell Staircase – painted in 1801 – is not half so much fun.

Burghley's flowery formal gardens were swept away in the 1750s by 'Capability' Brown. In went oaks, beeches, limes, chestnuts, a serpentine lake and broad sweeps of grass. But all this has done no harm; it is one of Brown's best landscapes.

78

Hatfield House, Hertfordshire
17th–19th century

TL 237084. Off junction 4, A1 (M), at Old Hatfield, on E side of A1000
[A]

Hatfield was built for Robert Cecil, Chief Minister of State, a rich, powerful,

Hatfield House, the Grand Staircase. AFK

intellectual man with a fondness for vast brick houses. In 1607 Cecil abandoned his Old Palace at Hatfield and began building a new house on a more prominent site. His aim was to woo royalty and stun everyone else. He took a keen personal interest in the building of the house and consulted various

architects and friends about it. The chief amongst these was probably Robert Lyminge, a carpenter who went on soon afterwards to build Blickling Hall (76, N).

Hatfield is an E-plan house, with two large brick wings linked by an Italianate stone loggia with a splendid three-store rontispiece dressed up with Doric, Ionic nd Corinthian columns. The date 1611 s carved in bold lettering on its parapet. Above rises an ornate clock tower. All his is typical Jacobean classicism; that ready mix of Gothic, Flemish and Italian Renaissance features. The wings, one of which contained the King's Lodgings, he other the Queen's Lodgings, each nave two corner towers with ogee tops. The whole front is symmetrical and aligned with a broad drive. The back of he house, by comparison, is severely plain. Hatfield, like Layer Marney Towers (83, E) was a grand gesture, a glorious piece of theatre with nothing backstage but bare walls. It was all done o impress.

Inside, despite 19th-century alterations, there is a profusion of Jacobean woodwork. A hall was still, as it had been all through the Middle Ages, he most important room in any large house; a communal space for meeting, holding court, junketing and feasting. The Hall is panelled and has two galleries (which is rare) lavishly carved with scallops, escutcheons and outlandish figures. The note struck here continues in the Grand Staircase. This is sumptuous. Freely adapted from Renaissance examples it rises in an easy-going way. Its balusters, newels, strings nd landings are richly carved. The newels are crowned with wooden figures some fierce, others sensual. Lions support heraldic devices, small muscular cherubs with big heads and highs wield symbolic objects or puff nto musical instruments. One post hows a bat with large ears, another the dainty figure of a gardener. The wooden gates were provided to stop dogs making a nuisance of themselves. The lighting is superb. Upstairs, the most magnificent room is the Long Gallery, again plushly panelled and decorated with strapwork nd classical motifs. It is 180 ft (54.8 m) ong, and has two ornate wooden fireplaces. Those who were not a-hunting could exercise and parade here, n this fashionable status symbol of a room.

East of the Long Gallery lies the royal suite. Cecil hoped James I would come nd stay at Hatfield and King James's Drawing Room contains an elaborate

fireplace with a life-size statue of the king perched on top. The ceiling is patterned in strapwork with pendants like giant iced-gems.

Hatfield's grounds have been much altered, although the eastern gardens imitate work done here in the 17th century. West of the house lies one range of the late 15th-century Old Palace, its buckled red brick looking ancient and crude beside Cecil's stately new building. Elizabeth I lived in the Old Palace when she was young and thereafter Cecil tactfully refrained from demolition. Hatfield displays a couple of flattering portraits of the great queen, as well as her garden hat and silk stockings.

79

Holkham Hall, Norfolk
18th century

TF 884428. 2 miles (3.2 km) W of Wells-next-the-Sea off A149

[A]

Art, time and expense created Holkham Hall. In 1712 a youthful Thomas Coke, Earl of Leicester, set out upon a Grand Tour which lasted six years. He ransacked the Continent for books, paintings, prints, antique sculptures. He developed a keen interest in architecture. In Italy he met William Kent, an English painter, and they toured together for a while, looking at buildings and scenery.

Coke returned to England and began landscaping a park on reclaimed saltmarsh and heath at Holkham, less than 1 mile (1.6 km) from the sea. In the early 1730s he began to build a new house and he persuaded Kent to help with the design. What emerged was 'a Burlington-house with four pavilions', in other words an up-to-date country house which owed much to the inspiration of Lord Burlington and the English Palladians. Holkham was designed along similar lines to Burlington's Chiswick Villa, London, and to Campbell's Houghton Hall (80, N). But whereas Chiswick was stuccoed and Houghton was stone, Holkham was built entirely of local snuff-coloured bricks and its builder was a Norfolk man, Mathew Brettingham.

In plan it consists of a central block with corner turrets linked to four outlying pavilions. Its main floor is raised above a rusticated basement. The chaste external walls have a compelling staccato rhythm of windows, pediments and setback angles. Each of the four pavilions is split into three pedimented blocks which is visually very satisfying. The great south portico has no steps and the main entrance is instead on the north front, through an unobtrusive doorway at basement level. Surely this was done to heighten the drama within? Through this doorway lies one of England's most splendid rooms. An entrance hall of startling originality, inspired by the Egyptian Hall of

Holkham Hall. CL

Vitruvius and the Venetian churches of Palladio, is formed by a ground-floor plinth of pink-veined alabaster, a gallery of operatically-scaled Ionic columns and a grand sweeping staircase rising to the piano nobile. The columns support an opulent frieze of cherubs, ox skulls and swags of fruit. The ceiling is deeply coffered. The effect is unforgettable; a silent fanfare for what follows.

Here is Kent at his most enchanting. Room follows room in a pavan-like succession of gorgeous furnishings and ceilings. Each one is different to the one before and each is of a rich and serene beauty. Coved, coffered, moulded, gilded, one with a frieze of griffins, another with vines, another with fruit, foliage, masks, another divided into deep panels, all picked out in white, gold and red. In the South Dining Room the temptation to grab a chair and await a splendid meal is difficult to resist. Amongst 18th-century interior designers Kent was *doyen exemplaire* and the visual ride, the experience of passing from one room into another is spellbinding. Windows frame the landscape – sheep-dotted, edged with trees and seemingly limitless. Outside and inside merge together; the house has become a tabernacle, space has become tangible and the visitor is the real focus of the space.

80

Houghton Hall, Norfolk
18th century

TF 793283. 10 miles (16 km) W of Fakenham off A148

[A]

Robert Walpole was a Norfolk man of great culture, industry and political skill. He was England's first Prime Minister. In 1722 he began Houghton Hall, an important and splendid example of English Palladianism. His architect was Colen Campbell – Scottish lawyer turned architect and arch-propagandist of the Palladian movement. Campbell published an influential book called *Vitruvius Britannicus* which shows designs for Houghton Hall which were largely carried out.

Houghton Hall, the west front. AFK

The house consists of a main block with two service wings linked by quadrant colonnades. The main block has four corner towers or pavilions, which were originally intended to have pedimented roofs but were later given small Continental-looking domes by James Gibbs. The overall impression of symmetry, order and harmony made Houghton hugely influential in the 1740s and 1750s; its greatest progeny was Holkham Hall (79, N).

Houghton is built from a silvery-grey sandstone which comes from Yorkshire but looks good in quiet Norfolk parkland. Like Holkham, Houghton was built for display and as a 'house of parade'; a place for occasion-making and rowdiness. A couple of times a year Walpole held 'congresses' at Houghton: hunting, gossiping, flirting, eating – boozing parties to which government cronies and local gentry were invited; mixed gatherings of the kind lampooned so mercilessly in Sheridan's plays. It was a clever way for Walpole to tame political society, exert influence, and keep a finger on the nation's pulse. Much of this worthwhile activity went on in 'the rustic', the lower storey living area. The posh storey above, the piano nobile, was intended more for looking at; gawping at really, given its breathtaking splendours.

There are four matching apartments in the piano nobile. When they were 'down in the country' Walpole and his wife lived in the eastern apartments which were separated from the western side by the Stone Hall and the Saloon. Both these rooms were extravagantly decorated. Much of the interior was the work of William Kent. No expense was spared. The great Stone Hall is a two-storey cube of unrivalled Palladian panache. The boldness of everything here – bracketed balcony, doorways, sumptuous fireplace with Roman relief, caryatids, guilloche – is stunning. The ceiling rests on a cove around which turnip-faced cherubs race, clamber and fall; one grabs hold of a busty sphinx, another charges around the chandelier. Below, classical busts sneer from the wall and two languid figures pose on a pediment above the entrance door. All frozen solid in stone, in piquant contrast to the Saloon which glitters with gilt and red Genoa velvet. Everywhere there is excellent craftsmanship: in the door-cases, in the mahogany Great Staircase, in the alcoves of the Marble Parlour (Walpole's dining room) and in the decoration of the Green Velvet Bedchamber. Few country houses display such quality and completeness.

Houghton's stable block has a matching grandeur. Inside there is faultless brick vaulting, original wooden stalls and the reek of horses and leather – a real whiff of 18th-century England.

81

Houghton House, Bedfordshire
17th century

TL 039395. ¾ mile (1.2 km) N of Ampthill off B530

[A] EH

Houghton House is an enigma. Not much is known about it or its architects. It stands high on a wind-struck hill overlooking the Bedfordshire brick fields. Romantically decayed and open to the sky, Houghton still retains some hilly dignity. It was built of brick and stone and begun c.1615. Its first owner was the Countess of Pembroke, sister of the poet-courtier Sir Philip Sidney, whose *Arcadia* was written for her one idle summer. That association is a clue, for Houghton was a courtier house; a minor version of the Jacobean 'prodigy' type. In plan it is H-shaped. Originally it had two storeys above a high basement. There were four angle turrets which according to early 19th-century prints had pyramid roofs. The main roofline was given shaped gables – like Blickling (76, N) and Hatfield (78, H).

Two things make Houghton specially interesting: the house was two rooms deep and its hall was in the centre of the south front and was entered in its middle. This was not a common arrangement for early 17th-century houses which were usually only one room deep and kept the medieval arrangement of a hall entered at one end. Two frontispieces, one on the north, the other on the west side of the house, add to the puzzle. Both are classical arrangements stacked with columns, arched windows, niches and entablatures, all done in stone. Frontispieces like these usually date from the 1630s and 1640s and not 1615. They are either very precocious original features or else they were put there a mere twenty years or so after Houghton was built. It has been suggested that they are by Inigo Jones, the flamboyant architect at Charles I's Court. If true then they are rare surviving examples of this great master's work.

Houghton was scrapped in the 1790s by its then owner the Duke of Bedford who had no use for it; an unworthy fate for the place which appears transformed in Bunyan's *Pilgrim's Progress*. He called it 'House Beautiful' which stood on 'Hill Difficulty'.

82

Ickworth House, Suffolk
18th–20th century

TL 816614. 3 miles (4.8 km) SW of Bury St Edmunds off A143

[A] NT

Ickworth is a sublime folly, a great tea-caddy of a house designed as a 'temple' to display the art collection of its builder, Frederick Hervey. Third son of a Royal Chamberlain, Hervey's early prospects were unexciting. He studied law but, after marrying, took holy orders. In 1768, at the age of 38, he was appointed Bishop of Derry in Ireland. From then onwards he flourished and was able to indulge his insatiable taste for travel, art and architecture. He had some eccentric ideas. One of them, which became an obsession, was to build a great oval mansion. As a trial run he got John Soane to design a circular dog kennel for him. He soon went on to bigger things. In 1786 he began to build a domed oval palace in Ireland. He abandoned it, returned to his family estate in Suffolk and in 1796 began another big oval at Ickworth. Frederick Sandys, an Irish architect, was left in charge of the actual building while Hervey roamed Europe in search of 'mosaick pavements, sumptuous chimney-pieces for my new house, marbles without end.'

Ickworth was designed as a large rotunda linked by one-storey curved wings to two-storey pavilions. The house is symmetrical in appearance. The rotunda, which is 100 ft (30.4 m) high, is domed and has two orders of attached columns wrapped around it; Ionic below, Corinthian above. Two terracotta friezes of classical figures, designed by Flaxman, run around the outside walls. Entrance to the house is by a large Ionic portico on the north front. The whole lot was built of brick coated with stucco after 'dear impeccable Palladio's rule', as Hervey wrote to his daughter. Despite this exciting project, foreign adventures kept Hervey away from Suffolk. In 1798 he was trapped in Rome by the invading French, his collection was confiscated and he was imprisoned. Freed the following year, he kept going, driven by *folie de grandeur* and his passion for collecting. Ickworth was still far from complete when he died in a peasant's hovel in Italy in 1803.

In the 1820s Hervey's second son laid out the gardens, patched up the rotunda for entertainments and built the wings for accommodation. The rooms are simply decorated in colours ranging from sombre coffee and yellow to off-white and mid-purple-brown. Inside, the eye is forever trying to straighten out

Houghton House. EH

Ickworth House from the south. AFK

the curves: there are intriguing glimpses through doorways into other rooms with rounded walls and high, coved ceilings.

The Hall is a monumental remodelling of 1909 by Sir Reginald Blomfield. Its two large columns frame Flaxman's contorted 'Fury of Athamas' sculpture. Behind lies the staircase, a design loaded with powerful tensions. Its ceiling threatens to crush the ascending visitor, and oversized roundels yawn across the open gulf of the stairwell. The sudden expanse of the landing offers some relief; but overhead balloons the never-completed space inside the dome – whitewashed brick, iron rods, exposed timbers, and a terrifying spiral staircase winding upwards.

Downstairs there is a curious Pompeian Room of 1879 lit by a small dome and decorated with Victorian 'Roman' wall-paintings. The Dining

Room decorations and furnishings date from the 1820s. The Library has impressive two-column screens at either end and a fireplace probably sent back from Rome by Bishop Hervey. He never lived at Ickworth but his restless nature still seems to imbue the atmosphere of this unfinished, extraordinary house.

83

Layer Marney Towers, Essex
16th century

TL 928175. 6 miles (9.6 km) SW of Colchester, 1 mile (1.6 km) S of B1022

[A]

Spectacular gatehouse towers were a feature of Tudor England. They occur at East Barsham (N), Oxburgh (N),

Buckden (C) and at Christ's, Trinity and St John's colleges in Cambridge (93, C). But nowhere are they as big or as blazing as at Layer Marney. This is a glamorous, luxurious tower, which shouts out 'Look at me!'.

It was built by Sir Henry Marney, Captain of the King's Bodyguard, Sheriff of Essex, Keeper of the Privy Seal. In 1520 this valiant knight accompanied Henry VIII to the fantastic European peace conference known as the Field of the Cloth of Gold. He brought some of the glory back to Essex in the early 1520s when he began to build a great mansion of which only the gatehouse tower and part of a west wing were ever completed.

The tower looks out over quiet, flat countryside. Designed for domestic accommodation it is built of brick, that colourful flexible material much loved in the 16th century. Its decorative features are of terracotta. The style is that which used to be called English Renaissance – a strange confection of late Gothic forms arded over with classically derived motifs, the whole thing as spicy as Tudor cookery. It was an acquired taste which started with the arrival in England of Italian craftsmen brought over by courtiers to produce tombs, toys and other decorative pieces. The pick-and-mix of motifs is especially noteworthy at Layer Marney. The plan, the polygonal turrets, the pointed arch windows and moulded brick arcading are typically English; the ornate terracotta windows and the lively parapet decorations of sliced fruit and dolphins are 15th-century Italian, derived from antiquity. Similar motifs appear on the monument to Henry Marney in the brick church nearby.

Wimpole Hall. NC

Why the English went in for these do-it-yourself classical features is not always clear, but it was done with great passion and gusto in these early years. People like Henry Marney wanted to prove that an age of secular building could still draw some gasps. He followed the antiquity theme through into the part of the west wing which was built before he died; two ceilings and a fireplace display more borrowings from Italy. After the bold and grand front the back of the tower comes as a shock; it is very plain, which is typical of England in all ages.

84
Wimpole Hall, Cambridgeshire
18th–19th century

TL 336510. 6 miles (9.6 km) N of Royston, signposted off A603

[A] NT

Wimpole is as good a place as any to study English architecture. It was begun in 1641 by the royalist, Thomas Chicheley, along lines which were becoming well established for country houses. The central block, although altered, is his. In the early 18th century James Gibbs, a baroque architect, remodelled the house and added wings; one containing the Library, the other the Chapel. Henry Flitcroft, a Palladian architect, re-faced the house, put in the Venetian and Diocletian windows and added a new front door in the 1740s. In

Layer Marney Towers, the gatehouse. AFK

the 1840s the house was extended yet again by H E Kendall, but much of his work has been demolished.

It is a surprise to enter the house, turn right and gaze down into the Chapel which is hidden behind the domestic-looking exterior. The Chapel is grand and in the tradition of Hampton Court. Thornhill painted it in *trompe l'oeil*, with squares of chocolate coffering and niches with grey Church Fathers. Melancholy light slants down through windows in the south wall.

In the 1790s came John Soane, master of space and purveyor of queer marine effects in architecture. He partly remodelled Gibbs's staircase, probably

adding the skylight. That is harmless enough. So too are the arched Book Rooms which he created in the Library wing. A small bathroom cleverly fitted in behind a service staircase may also be by Soane. Its claustrophobic plunge bath (which has water in it) was used for invigorating cold dips and provides evidence of the early 19th-century's growing preoccupation with 'services' in country houses, in this case plumbing.

But nothing prepares the visitor for Soane's Yellow Drawing Room. This is powerful stuff. In plan it is two squares; one with a tunnel vault, the other with apses and a dome with a lantern on top. It was intended for grand receptions,

balls and concerts. Its walls are lined with sultry yellow silk, and the wan light falling from above creates a dream-like atmosphere. This is a room like a sea-urchin's shell; fragile and poetic like so much of Soane's work.

Flitcroft designed the Gallery and rebuilt the church in the grounds in 1749. Kendall built the huge red and white stable block with its glib cupola in 1851. Charles Bridgeman was here in the 1720s and 'Capability' Brown in the 1760s; both of them landscaping the park. Repton came in 1801–9 and made alterations. Sanderson Miller created the deliciously deceiving Gothic ruin away across the fields to the north.

9

Landscapes, Parks and Gardens

Landscapes, parks, gardens and forests developed in eastern England as elsewhere, for pleasure, entertainment and hunting. From the Middle Ages, only slices of the once vast royal forests remain. **Hatfield Forest** (85, E) is the best example. An oak-filled deer park survives at Helmingham Hall (S). Layer Marney (83, E) had one and Braxted Park's (E) dates from the mid-13th century. There were extensive gardens, orchards and vineyards at St Albans Abbey (24, H) and at Ely (21, C) by the 11th century, but these have vanished along with the walled and jewel-like country-house gardens, made for rose-growing and courtly love.

In Tudor and Stuart times substantial deer parks were created at Burghley (77, C), Wimpole (84, C) and most splendidly at Woburn (B). The gardens which accompanied such parks were formal and in the case of those made for the 'prodigy houses', grandly geometrical and closely related to the architecture. The knot and the maze were favourite 16th-century features. In the 17th century, gardens became more sophisticated – waterworks, walks, canals and elaborate *parterres* were fashionable. Grottoes began to appear: early examples were often in the basement of a country house like that at Woburn (B); later ones were out in the garden, like **Scott's Grotto, Ware** (87, H). Gardens grew larger and spread further into the countryside; grand avenues in the French manner were popular by the late 17th century. The house stood at the centre with symmetrical walks and vistas stretching away in all directions. **Wrest Park** (90, B) retains some of this formal scale and grandeur with its Long Water and view-stopping Pavilion. **St Paul's Walden Bury** (86, H) is a very late example dating from the 1730s; a rare and beautiful conjunction of nature and art.

The 18th-century landscape garden was an English invention, literary in

origin, painterly and sublime in effect. It went hand-in-hand with Palladianism's strict formality in architecture. The idea was to re-create the landscape of the Italian *campagna* where English tourists saw the paintings of Salvator Rosa, Claude and Poussin become real in the bright Italian sunshine. Fired with the vision of a lyrical countryside dotted with ruined temples, they set about creating similar scenes at home. At Holkham Hall (79, N), William Kent made a landscape of distant prospects where garden and park melt into one.

'Capability' Brown took things further. He re-shaped Kent's work at Holkham before going on to 'improve' or influence most of the major country parks in England. His impact was enormous. Old formal gardens, irritating hills, rivers, even entire villages were swept away to make room for his creations. He worked at Moor Park (H), Ickworth (82, S), Audley End (75, E), Wrest Park, Luton Hoo (B), Ashridge (74, H), Wimpole Hall (84, C) and Burghley (77, C), where he spent thirty years forming a huge lake and moving massive trees around. Brown had great ideas for the Cambridge Backs, but only King's College with its open lawns and pastures look anything like his designs. The rest of the riverside colleges kept their enclosed gardens, which are now laid out in 20th-century fashion.

Humphry Repton followed Brown, contriving ever more picturesque effects on the large-scale and variety and detail on the small-scale. At Woburn (B) he complemented Henry Holland's Chinese Dairy by adding a Chinese garden and menagerie. At Holkham and at Ashridge he 'revised' Brown's work. **Sheringham Park** (88, N), set by the sea amidst heath and cornfields, was his greatest achievement.

In the 19th century the great tradition of the landscaped *jardin anglais* began to falter. Other influences began to reappear. Wrest Park was given

The rose garden, Luton Hoo. AFK

The 1950s temple, Anglesey Abbey. AFK

a magnificent French *parterre* in the 1830s; Shrubland Park (S) was given huge Italian terraces and flights of steps in the 1840s. Picturesque rock-work, gloomy valleys and dogs' graveyards crept in along with the revival styles. A 17th-century maze was re-created at Hatfield House (78, H) and Somerleyton Hall (S) given formal gardens to go with its neo-Jacobean appearance. Interesting gardens appeared in odd places, like the **Swiss Garden and Old Warden Village** (89, B) an eclectic mixture of allsorts, or the more modest Bridge End Gardens, Saffron Walden (E).

The 20th century has left its own colours and impressions. Luton Hoo gained an Edwardian rose garden with Indian temples. A beautiful Japanese garden was begun at Cottered (H) in the 1920s. Country houses had their gardens added to or replanted. From 1930 onwards the grounds of Anglesey Abbey were developed with stately avenues, temples and garden statuary, often in celebration of some splendid event, like the Coronation of Queen Elizabeth II. The Botanic Gardens in Cambridge (C) have carried out important work. The most spectacular 20th-century planting is in the garden cities of Letchworth (H) and Welwyn Garden City (H). The New Towns are a typically English mixture – an urban 'sharawaggi' of modern architecture and 18th-century landscape gardening.

96

85
Hatfield Forest, Essex

TL 547203. Off junction 8, M11, S of A120 between Great Hallingbury and Takeley

[A] NT

This is the only place in England where all the features of a medieval forest can be seen. There are woodland trees, plains with scrubs and ancient thorns, deer, cattle and a rabbit warren.

In the Middle Ages a forest was not just an oversized fairytale wood; it was a place inhabited by the king's game. It had its own special laws and administration and it included farmland, woodland, villages and even towns. Until the start of the 14th century the Forest of Essex covered most of the county. Two shrunken fragments remain today; Epping and Hatfield Forests.

Hatfield Forest covers over 1,000 acres (404.7 ha). Most of its elms have been wiped out but there are oaks, hornbeams, sweet and horse chestnuts. The landscape varies from close coppice to broad green plains and patches of marsh. The 18th-century 'improvements' included rides, a lake and a lakeside pavilion, the Shell House, a semi-grotto built by the Houblon family who owned the Forest from 1446 until the 1920s. Two other buildings, Forest Lodge and Warren Lodge, were built at different times for a forester and a warren-keeper.

Hatfield Forest. P ROGERS/ECC

Hatfield's woodland has always needed careful management. Selective felling and coppicing were early and important developments in the supply of timber for building. Suitable trees, sixty to 100 years old and grown straight, were felled in the autumn and carted or dragged away to building sites in local Essex towns like Saffron Walden, Thaxted and Great Dunmow. The economics of timber conversion were neither straightforward nor cheap, but from little acorns grew mighty oaks and from their timbers came houses, churches, barns, bridges and Ships-of-the-Line. Hearts of Oak was a reality, not just an English folk-song.

At the beginning of the 16th century, there were about 4 million acres (1.6 million ha) of woods and forests in England. Teeming with game, noisy with the sounds of hunting, sawing and farming, an English forest was a busy place. Two dates plucked from history bring Hatfield to life: in 1328 'John' the blacksmith had the right to go into the Forest each year and help himself to the second best oak tree, which he did without fail; in 1630 one 'Thomas Clark a wandering fellowe' was employed to 'cutt grasse in the coppices at 1*d*. a bundle'. The coarse grass still grows in Hatfield Forest.

86
St Paul's Walden Bury Garden, Hertfordshire
18th–20th century

TL 187217. 5 miles (8 km) S of Hitchin off B651 between St Paul's Walden and Whitewell

[A]

An enchanted grove, a place for nymphs and shepherds. One of the last great French-inspired gardens in England, laid out by Edward Gilbert in the 1730s. Its framework is a formal kite-shaped series of walks or *allées* running northwards from the early 18th-century house. These long hedge-lined *allées* are cut through mature woods of oak, hornbeam and beech and end with view-stoppers; a statue of Hercules, a hunting

t Paul's Walden Bury. CL

irl and two dogs, a Venus and Adonis,
n exquisite white-painted temple. One
llée is cleverly aligned on the tower of
ne village church which remains
hrunk to the size of an ornament until
ecognised (with a gasp) for what it is.

The most exciting and unusual
eature is a happy accident: the ground
ndulates dramatically. Few formal
ardens were provided with such natural
oetry. Trees and grass surge away from
ne house, dip downwards and then race
wiftly up again. The effect is lyrical.

Half-way along the main *allée*,
idden away to one side is the Theatre of
ne Running Footman, a tranquil glade
creened by trees and boxy hedges. From
silent pool of water a lawn swirls
pwards to a small temple. It is a rare
xample of a *giardino segreto*, a
winsome, lonely garden-within-a-
arden.

A great garden is a living thing. Work
f later years overlays the early planning
f St Paul's Walden Bury. There are
8th-century alterations, a strait-laced
ictorian terrace near the house and
reer 1930s-style flower gardens. The
arge area of woodland lying to the west
vas developed this century and forms a
leasing contrast to the clipped hedges
nd cut-out walks. Formality merges
nto informality, gardens into pheasant-
otted farmland, the 20th century into
he spacious days of Georgian England.
t in Arcadia Ego.

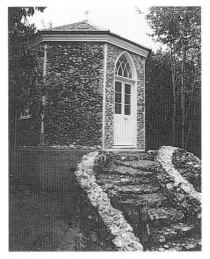

Scott's Grotto, the summerhouse. DPWS

87
Scott's Grotto, Ware, Hertfordshire
18th century

TL 356138. In Scott's Road, Ware,
off A119 Hertford Road
[A]

This place is fun. Dr Johnson called it 'a
Fairy Hall'. John Scott, its builder,
called it his 'Cavern or Subterraneous

Grot'. Quaker, poetaster, mild eccentric
and friend of the London literati, Scott
began his grotto in the 1760s in the back
garden of his house near Ware. Artificial
caverns or grottoes originated in Italy
and appear in England in the 17th
century as part of the love of things
Italian. They were especially fashionable
in the 18th century but few were as
extensive as this one. One of Scott's
poems refers to '. . . some secret shady
cool recess/some Gothic dome o'erhung
with darksome trees'; a private
underground place where he could take
candlelit walks.

A flint rubble porch leads to a suite of
six interlinking rooms. All the rooms are
circular except one and most of them
have occasional niches set into their
walls. Inside it is as dark as the grave.
There are subterranean junctions, voids
and narrow shafts giving glimpses of
other rooms. These seem inaccessible,
until after fumbling around, the visitor
suddenly finds himself inside one.
Almost every surface is covered by
shells, stones and minerals.

The most exotic room is the Council
Chamber. The floor is an elaborate swirl
of small pebbles and fifty different kinds
of shell cover the circular walls. Sea-
shells were an 18th-century fascination
and here are mother-of-pearl, Venus
ears, combs, sundials, pagodas, fans,
pale tigers and paper nautiluses,
wonderfully made and echoing with the
sound of distant seas.

Above ground, Scott added some
suitably rustic garden buildings. On top
of the hill an octagonal gazebo and a
garden seat in the form of a curious flint
sentry-box have been restored. These are
typical of the kind of picturesque
ornaments for which a real craze
developed in the late 18th and the 19th
centuries. Such gimcracks had a noble
ancestry in the paintings of Poussin and
Claude and the landscapes of Brown and
Repton.

Scott's Grotto is a home-made place
but that is part of its charm. It mingles
the pleasures of childhood exploration
with older instincts of the cave. It
titillates without being vulgar and it all
happens behind a boarded fence in a
dull, nicely ordered housing estate. That
makes it a folly as well as a grotto.

97

Small temple, Sheringham Park. NT

88

Sheringham Park, Norfolk
19th–20th century

TG 134424. 1 mile (1.6 km) SW of Sheringham off B1157

[A] NT

Sheringham Park is a perfect example of the English Landscape Tradition. Jane Austen could quite easily have used it as the setting for one of her novels. In *Mansfield Park* she actually mentions its designer, Humphry Repton. Repton, who was born in Bury St Edmunds (S), invented the term 'landscape gardening', although it was not until he was thirty-nine, after a failed business career, that he turned gardener to support his family. Between 1792 and 1816 he altered and 'improved' over 400 English parks and gardens. His success was partly due to his simple but exciting way of presenting ideas. He made watercolours of 'before' and 'after' his intended improvements and flapped one aside to reveal the other. Important clients received theirs bound in red leather as a 'Red Book'.

The 'Red Book' which he prepared for Abbot Upcher, owner of Sheringham Park, still exists. From the start Repton was delighted with the opportunity which Upcher gave him in 1812 to create a new landscape. The natural irregularity and variation of this part of

the Norfolk coast lent itself to picturesque planning. Ice Age glaciers had left Sheringham with an intricate landscape of shallow frost-free valleys and low wooded hills with the sea beyond them. Repton made great use of these natural accidents. At the same time his son, who often worked with him, designed a house of simple proportions for Upcher and his young wife. Its classical lines, cream-coloured bricks and grey slate roof form a pleasing contrast to the oak-covered hill behind and the open swathe of pasture in front. The house is reached by a woodland drive which winds through thickly planted rhododendrons sprinkled with conifers, beeches and sweet chestnuts.

At 'The Turn' the drive sweeps out of the woods to give a downhill view of the house, framed by trees and edged by cornfields and the sea. All this was carefully contrived. The only man-made object Repton allowed in the scheme was a small temple, but this was not built until the 20th century. It doubles up as an eye-catcher and a vantage point from which to overlook the undulating park and pastures. Amongst sixteen words chosen to describe the sources of pleasure in landscape gardening, Repton lists Picturesque Effect, Intricacy, Simplicity, Variety, Contrast, Continuity and The Seasons. All these are deliciously present at Sheringham and Repton always referred to it as his 'favourite work'.

89

Swiss Garden and Old Warden Village, Bedfordshire
19th–20th century

TL 148448. 2½ miles (4.8 km) W of Biggleswade off B658

[A]

A chocolate-box garden laid out by the 3rd Lord Ongley at the height of a minor craze for Swiss things in the 1820s, this is early 19th-century Picturesque landscaping – rustic, intimate, whimsically exotic. The inspiration may have been J B Papworth's *Hints on*

Ornamental Gardening (1823) which showed how to design an interesting setting for ornamental buildings. Crammed into 9 acres (3.6 ha) there is an exciting selection of trees, lawns, groves, sauntering paths, ponds and shrubberies. Deodar, incense, cedar, false acacia and the curious monkey puzzle, so beloved of the 19th century, are found here along with laurel, rhododendron, Swiss pine, oak and beech.

Two ponds, with islands scattered with urns and delicate humped iron bridges, occupy the northern corner of the garden. An Indian kiosk with bark and twig-work decoration loiters nearby. Walks meander away to a thatched Tree Shelter, an Italianate Well-Head, and a Garden House which owes its appearance perhaps to some wayside shrine glimpsed in Switzerland.

The grotto-cum-fernery combines a gloomy cave of tufa stone with an early cast-iron glasshouse. In the centre of the garden stands the rustic Swiss Cottage; a two-storeyed, fretted and thatched building with a verandah. It is delightfully of its time and doubtless served some practical use as a summer house or a place to take tea in. Gardens like this, with their ever-changing vistas and swings and turns, were made for hide-and-seek, for lovers and light-hearted intrigue.

There is a popular belief that Lord Ongley made the gardens to please his Swiss mistress. The same fanciful note is

Swiss Garden, the Swiss Cottage. NC

truck by the estate village which he created nearby. Old Warden is party-ioing Picturesque. Its planning and andscaping are expertly handled and attention to detail – rooflines, windows, orches, doors, bargeboards – is superb. olourwash and white paint are much in vidence. The whole village is knitted ogether by careful planting of hedges nd evergreens. P F Robinson, a leading icturesque architect, had done estate ork in Bedfordshire already and he may ave been responsible for these elightfully decorated cottages. But it as Lord Ongley who had the brilliant dea that his tenants should all wear red loaks and tall hats so as to 'harmonise ith their dwellings'.

00

Vrest Park Pavilion, Bedfordshire
8th century

L 093356. 1 mile (1.6 km) E of ilsoe off A6

A] EH

banqueting house set on a grassy hound at the end of a Long Water. This avilion, built for the 1st Duke of Kent n 1709–11, is one of the outstanding uildings of the English baroque school f architecture. Its architect Thomas rcher, born 1668, attended Oxford, did he Grand Tour, returned to England nd settled into the life-style of entleman-architect and successful ourtier. In the space of a few years he uilt three churches, two town houses nd worked on a couple of country ouses, including one for himself in lampshire. Although he was a Whig and Protestant, during his travels abroad rcher had developed an intense interest n the baroque architecture of Catholic taly. Wrest Pavilion betrays evidence of n intimate knowledge of the work of wo Italian masters of spatial effects; ernini and Borromini.

Between 1706 and 1740 the Duke of Kent was laying out the Great Garden at Vrest. Archer's pavilion was its focal oint. From here *allées* and rides radiate

Wrest Park pavilion. EH

outwards to intersect with intricate winding walks, enclosed clumps of trees and other garden buildings. The pavilion made a splendid view-stopper from the old Wrest House which stood closer to the Long Water than the present 1830s pile. But this pavilion is no garden ornament, despite its toy-like appearance from a distance. It is bigger and bolder than it looks and its voltage increases with every approaching step. Face-to-face, the sheer personality and presence of this domed *tempietto* come as a real shock.

In plan the pavilion is a hexagon with alternate round and square sides; a

memory of the strange shapes and restless spaces of Borromini's Roman churches. There are bull's-eye windows in the drum and the pediment over the entrance has three flaming urns. Inside there is a saloon with a brilliantly false coffered ceiling. The decoration in *trompe l'oeil* is by Nicholas Hauduroy, a Dutch artist.

Few buildings in England are as strikingly original as this pavilion. Yet within four years of its completion, at the height of his creative powers, Archer became Controller of Customs at Newcastle (a most lucrative post) and gave up architecture altogether.

10

Villages, Towns and Cities

Between Hertfordshire and Norfolk lies the England of villages, planned communities, garden cities, cathedral cities, river ports, coastal ports and New Towns. Within this large geographical area there is a rich variety of townscape and scenery, and many local differences.

Bedfordshire looks and feels remote for such a centrally placed county. It is a place of strong contrasts. There are workaday, unpretentious villages and tired-looking towns like Ampthill, Shefford and Biggleswade with a sober brick-faced character of their own. What Bedfordshire is best at are planned or model villages. Woburn and Old Warden (89, B) are picture-book examples put up for their estate workers by the powerful landowners. The Bedford estate built others at Husborne Crawley, Lidlington, Ridgmont and Willington. At Cardington Green, John Howard the philanthropist built several cottages in the 1760s. Later, Shorts built Shortstown for their workers who constructed giant airships. At **Stewartby** (100, B) the London Brick Company created a Model Village in the years between 1927 and the 1950s.

Hertfordshire, unlike Bedfordshire, is almost completely gentrified. To the south, Watford, Rickmansworth and 'Metroland', merge into London. This is suburbia at its ripest. St Albans is big, expensive and knocked about, like its cathedral. Hertford retains some of the atmosphere of a country town with a good mix of urban vernacular buildings. Beyond lie the sleek villages of east Hertfordshire; the Hadhams, the Pelhams, the Hallingburys, full of prettily restored cottages. Baldock and Buntingford are small towns with almshouses and 18th- and 19th-century brick buildings. The chalkland villages of north Hertfordshire are rich in houses and cottages made of traditional materials; plaster covered timber-framing, cob, chalk-lump and white bricks. **Ashwell** (91, H) is one which retains its sense of place. Towns with a strong identity in

Hertfordshire are **Letchworth** (96, H) and Welwyn Garden City, the world's first 'garden cities'. The New Towns of Hatfield, Hemel Hempstead and Stevenage belong to that brave post-Second World War rebuilding period.

Essex got its new town in Harlow, where England's first modern tower block, The Lawns, was built. Harlow was landscaped along 18th-century lines, kept a 'traditional' market in its windy new centre and got a fire station like a child's toy. Essex is a big and diverse county; its Thames-side is grim, its north-west corner is idyllic, with woods, gently rolling pea and corn fields and small towns and villages. Saffron Walden (the best medieval town in Essex), Thaxted and the Bardfields are crammed with timber-framing, cream-and-white plaster, old red tiles and thatch. Pargeting, the folk art of making pictures in the street by moulding and shaping the plaster on walls, is a speciality. Big inland towns are few: Colchester (5, E) has Roman walls, a stunning town hall (48, E), a 'Dutch Quarter' and streets of fine Georgian houses; Chelmsford is dull. Character returns with the eastern river ports and old malting towns of Maldon, Manningtree and Mistley (**Stour Valley**, 101, E, S), which has a working wharf, church towers designed by Robert Adam and a fountain with a large swan in the middle. Wivenhoe is a place of jolly, bow-windowed houses and boats. Harwich is a ghost town, with packed-in buildings and intriguing nooks and corners. Frinton was once teetotal and has the largest collection of Modern Movement houses in England. Whelk-and-pier towns like Clacton and Southend were smart Edwardian resorts and are still lively and crowded on Bank Holidays. Essex has one notable estate village – Silver End, the Crittalls equivalent of Stewartby. It has unusual inter-war modern houses; squared, flat roofed and originally white; now ice-cream coloured.

Queen's College, Cambridge, from The Backs.
FK

Flatford Mill. JC

Suffolk is rolling and pastoral; the England of Vaughan Williams and Britten, sprinkled with colourwashed villages and small market towns. Ipswich, the largest town, has some outstanding buildings and a varied townscape; docks, quayside and warehouses and a network of narrow medieval streets. Lowestoft developed as a canal and fishing port and still manages a striking jumble of boats, houses and railways. Suffolk's most rewarding town, architecturally, is Bury St Edmunds, with its fine quality Georgian brickwork, well-preserved street patterns and market hall by Adam. Woodbridge has riverside yards and sail lofts. Beccles and Bungay are honest and hard-working, the latter with a rustic, domed Butter Cross.

Norwich, Octagon Chapel. JB

Long Melford, Clare and **Lavenham** (95, S) are medieval wool towns with splendid churches and buildings; cluttered together in Lavenham, strung out in Long Melford and Clare. Coastal towns in Suffolk are different from those in Essex or Norfolk. At **Southwold**

(99, S) and Aldeburgh there are shingle beaches, fishing-tackle sheds and striped bathing huts. Houses have wooden or iron balconies and bow windows to catch the marine light. **Somerleyton** (98, S) is a 19th-century Model Village. Newmarket, on the Cambridgeshire border, is given over to horses.

Cambridgeshire, as Defoe noted, means **Cambridge** (93, C), the great university with a unique riverside known as The Backs. Most of the county is Fen; a huge slice of land, drained, farmed, sparsely inhabited and dead flat. There are dead towns too, like March, Littleport and Chatteris, and beaten-up villages with subsiding roadside chapels. The heart of the Fen is Ely, a small city dominated by a big cathedral (21, C). In Cambridgeshire's eastern corner lies **Wisbech** (102, C) and the most splendid Georgian riverscape in England.

The Fens extend into Norfolk and between Wisbech and the ancient port of **King's Lynn** (94, N) there is marshland, an area of nondescript villages with boldly silhouetted churches. Mid-Norfolk undulates gently and is scattered with towns like East Dereham, Wymondham and Swaffham, with its thriving market and domed 'cross' with

Lavenham, houses at the junction of Water Street and Lady Street. JB

res on top. **Norwich** (97, N) is the
rgest town in East Anglia with
thedral, castle, market, medieval
urches, civic and commercial
ildings, narrow streets of houses and a
ver. East of here lie the Broads, with
eir holiday villages, ruined wind-
mps and lakes occasionally crossed by
anch line railways. In Loddon and
ighbouring villages England's best
ural council housing was built in the
st-Second World War years: crisp,
ricultural rows of houses with fields
lling right up to their back gardens. In
e 1950s this housing attracted world-
ide attention.

North Norfolk is picturesque in the
8th-century sense. There is intricacy
nd roughness in the dusty lanes, the
er-changing light, the roadside stacks
beet and turnip, the variations in the
ndscape. Brick, flint and pantiles are
e materials here and along the coast in
lakeney (92, N), Cley, Morston and
althouse there are houses faced with
a-washed pebbles and topped with
utch gables'.

Sheringham and Cromer are bucket-
nd-spade towns, poignant with
minders of the English seaside: a once-
and hotel in the French style, vying
reets of flint and terracotta guest
ouses, kiosks on Cromer pier, a lifeboat
ation, a lighthouse, faded deck chairs. A
w miles inland, wearing an abandoned
r is Melton Constable, built as a
ilway village at a great interchange of
nes and now stranded amongst fields.

The 'Holy Land' of Walsingham,
ached by many winding lanes, is the
d of pilgrimages past and present: a
range, serious place of shrines, ruins
nd plastic saints. Henry VIII, Erasmus
nd T S Eliot came here. The former
reat Eastern Railway station is now a
ussian Orthodox church; a small onion
ome glints above the old ticket office.

Ashwell, the Wells. JC

1

shwell, Hertfordshire

L 268397. 6 miles (9.6 km) NE of
aldock off A505

he village of Ashwell has managed to
reserve a strong sense of its medieval

character in spite of a devastating fire in
the mid-19th century. On the north
side, fields lap up against the village
boundary and there are still farmsteads
in the village. It developed around the
long High Street with a market place in
the centre, defined by Swan Street to the
north. From there, Mill Lane runs down
by the church meadow to the river, and
loops back past the medieval Duck Lake
Farm.

A convenient starting place is the
Wells, at the east end of the High Street.
The limpid pool which bubbles up
through a series of fissures in the chalk
is the source of the River Rhee, one of
the main tributaries of the Cam.
Encircled by ash trees, it is also the
source of the village's name. The Saxons
knew it as Aescwellan but its origins may
be much older for the ash tree and the
well were sacred to pagan religion. The

103

prehistoric Icknield Way runs close by the village. The Domesday survey listed Ashwell, the property of the Abbot of Westminster, with its market and four annual fairs in the top ten of the county's towns.

The local geology is one of undulating chalk downs, which were once heavily wooded, with deposits of glacial clay in the river valleys. Timber, brick, clay-lump and clunch, imbue it with characteristics from each of the neighbouring counties. In the High Street are a number of medieval timber-framed hall-houses with jettied cross-wings, most rendered externally like the Rose and Crown pub. St John's Guildhall is a long jettied range with the studding exposed, and next door is some rustic decorative plasterwork, or pargeting, dated 1681. Further on, the medieval origins of Bear House are revealed by its arched doorway and glimpses of mullioned windows. The Town House with its medieval shopfront was built during the 15th century in the market place to collect the abbot's tolls and dues, and was restored as a museum in 1929.

Use of 18th-century red brick, chequered with burnt brick headers, makes an appearance at the top of the High Street in The Three Tuns Hotel and Jessamine House. The Merchant Taylors School of 1681 opposite the church is of mellow, mottled buff brick. Cambridgeshire gault, a creamy brick which became fashionable around 1800, is used for a number of good villas and the modest Zoar Baptist Chapel with its little walled graveyard in Gardiners Lane. Clay-lump was used for humbler cottages, both on its own and combined with a smarter brick front. Always plastered externally for protection, it can be detected by the thickness of the wall. In Gardiners Lane it appears in the raw in the form of a thatched wall. The tiny town lock-up in Hodwell, with its heavily studded door, is built of huge, badly weathered blocks of clunch.

At the churchyard entrance is a rare timber double lych gate of the 15th century with a crown post roof. The 14th-century flint and clunch built church, with its 176 ft (53.6 m) high tower crowned with an octagonal lantern and spike, is the most ambitious in the county. Inside the tower some rare and poignant Latin graffiti commemorating the Black Death translates: '1350, wretched, fierce, violent. The dregs of the populace live to tell the tale . . . a mighty wind . . . thunders in the heavens 1361'.

92
Blakeney, Norfolk

TG 030436. On A149 coast road, 5 miles (8 km) NW of Holt

Along the North Norfolk coast there are small villages built of flint and brick.

Salthouse, Cley, Wiveton, Burnham, Blakeney, were once busy ports, trading in wool and agricultural produce with London and the Continent. Now they are separated from the sea by shallow waters, sand and marsh. Blakeney was one of the larger ports. In the Middle Ages it had a Carmelite friary, boat-building yards and warships. A great Perpendicular church, battered and salt-stung, still dominates the village. The smaller of its two towers acts as landmark by day and lighthouse by night, combining romance and practicality in true nautical style. The symbolism of saving souls was not lost upon a community whose lives were closely linked with boats and the sea.

Blakeney, the High Street, c. 1900. NLIS

The village lies below the church, most of it packed along the meandering High Street where the intricate mix of buildings, mostly of the 18th and 19th centuries, is a real delight. Tiny, tatty cottages rub up against double-fronted merchants' houses. Narrow alleys lead off towards sheds, outbuildings and rows of one-and-a-half storey cottages huddled round secret-looking yards. Flint grips the eye everywhere. Buildings, walls, gateways, street edging, bollards, are all made of beach-gathered cobbles. Some houses have their side walls done in different sized cobbles to their fronts, and here and there a daintier note is struck by panels of small pebbles no larger than hens' eggs. Red brick dressings, pantiles, trees, hollyhocks and paint add further detail and variety. Painting houses is a coastal tradition and there are houses here with walls and windows in different colours; black and white, pink and white, green and white, and glorious yellow and blue.

Going downhill, the High Street suddenly kinks sideways to reveal at its far end the Quay; an unplanned slice of scenic excitement, where the immediacy of water, boats and sky is perfectly expressed. A jumble of mooring posts, masts, steps and hand-painted ferry signs contrasts with steeply roofed former warehouses and a bland 1920s hotel along the front. On high tides weatherbeaten fishing smacks and snug cruisers ride alongside the footpath. A low, red and white Georgian house closes the view at one end of the Quay. At the other end, set back across the road, lie the vaulted remains of some 15th-century merchant's house. The nearby mound is man-made, a spyglass hill which once sported a cannon to discourage pirates, or the French.

From up here can be seen the lonely watch-house across the mud flats in the distance. It stood close to the entrance to the harbour, now silted up and suitable only for sailing gaily coloured dinghies.

Looking back from a boat, or from the wind-scoured beaches of Blakeney Point, the village takes on fresh meaning: a landmark and safe haven for mariners, a place of salt-marsh, crabs, cockles and memorable summers; a scribble of pantiled roofs like shorthand for the sea which is never far away.

93
Cambridge, Cambridgeshire

TL 450585.

Cambridge is a unique anthology of English architecture where century after century can be measured by the buildings, their details and materials. It is, too, an illustrious university and a busy city, its centre splashed with a colourful market and bounded by open spaces – Jesus Green, Midsummer Common, Christ's Pieces, The Backs – all hugged in and drawn tight by the River Cam.

In the wedge of townscape between Queen's Road and St Andrew's Street lies the heart of Cambridge. Here is the old city to which scholars from Oxford and Paris came to found colleges where students could be taught. There are endless surprises here. Strong contrasts are formed in scale and atmosphere, like that between the intimate churchyard and cottage groups and the college buildings which loom across the street or crowd along narrow alleys.

The anthology begins with 11th- and 12th-century fragments: the tower of St Bene't's Church, built before the Conquest; the rare Round Church of the Holy Sepulchre; the 'School of Pythagoras', which was once a private house. The first college building was the hall of Peterhouse, built in 1286, but the best example of a medieval college is Queen's Old Court of 1448–9, complete with gate-tower, lodgings, hall and chapel. The monastery-like arrangement of buildings reflects the discipline and ritual of early academic life: meals were eaten in hall, services attended in chapel and teaching was carried out within the college walls. Queen's College has a picturesque, half-timbered Cloister Court which dates from the 1540s and was the first cloister built in Cambridge.

Medieval colleges, like great medieval houses, had gate-towers; symbolic of authority and the defence of quiet courtyards behind them. Trinity, a large

and well-endowed college, has three lavish examples: King Edward's Tower (1427–37 and the oldest in Cambridge), Great Gate (1518–35 with a statue of Henry VIII holding a chair-leg) and Queen's Gate (1596–7 in the Great Courtyard which is the largest of any Oxbridge College). Christ's and St John's Colleges both have 16th-century gate-towers glittering with heraldry including roses, crowns and portcullises. These emblems recur in Cambridge's greatest medieval building, King's College Chapel (30, C).

Classical architecture began to arrive in Cambridge in the mid-16th century. The Gates of Virtue and of Honour at Gonville and Caius College date from then. The Gate of Honour is a quirky pepperpot, spiced with symbolism and much restored. Nevile's Hall at Trinity College, despite its date of 1604–5, still hankers after the Middle Ages with its great bay windows, hammerbeam roof and minstrels' gallery. Peterhouse Chapel, 1628–32, is a haunting mix of classical and late Gothic features. Shortly after this period Clare College began to be rebuilt along more refined lines. The river front of 1669–76 is especially memorable. By comparison the brick, Dutch-gabled Third Court of St John's (built at the same time) looks homely and old-fashioned.

Christopher Wren worked at Cambridge from the 1660s onwards. Pembroke College Chapel (1665) was actually his first completed building. Wren followed this classical essay with Emmanuel College Chapel, which is more baroque. His most brilliant Cambridge building is Trinity College Library (1676–95) faultlessly built in pink and honey-coloured stone, crisply detailed and accompanied by graceful arched cloisters. Wren's classicism led unerringly on to the 18th-century Palladianism of James Gibbs whose Senate House (1722–30) and Gibbs Building (1724–32) at King's College are icons of the Cambridge scene. Around the Senate House runs a thicket of blackberry-black iron railings which are amongst the earliest in England. Stephen Wright's 1750s front to Cobble Court shares the same lawn as the Senate House. Beyond to the right is the end of C R Cockerell's Old University Library, a large building crammed down one side of Senate House Passage. This library is neo-classical and dates from the 1830s, like Basevi's great Fitzwilliam Museum (although there the similarities end) which always appears absurdly foreshortened due to its site. These are university rather than college buildings

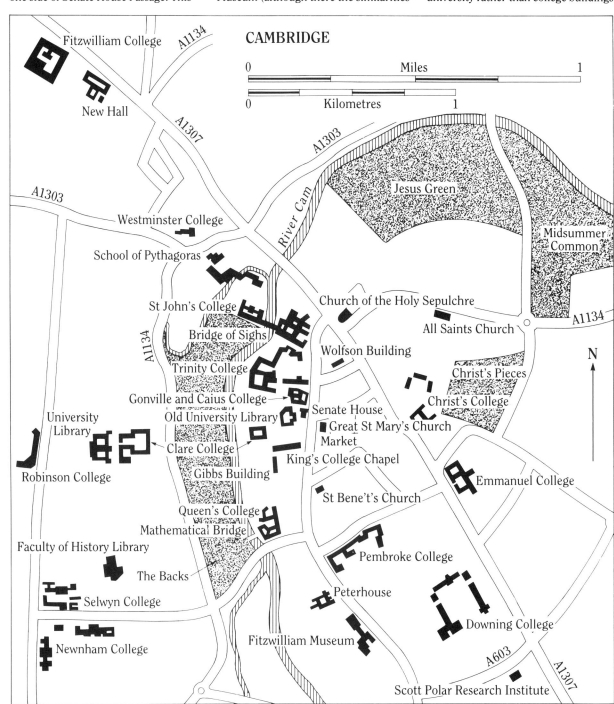

CAMBRIDGE

Fitzwilliam College
A1134
New Hall
A1307
A1303
Westminster College
School of Pythagoras
St John's College
Bridge of Sighs
A1134
Trinity College
Gonville and Caius College
Old University Library
University Library
Clare College
Robinson College
Gibbs Building
Queen's College
Mathematical Bridge
Faculty of History Library
The Backs
Selwyn College
Newnham College

River Cam
A1303
Jesus Green
Midsummer Common
A1134
Church of the Holy Sepulchre
All Saints Church
Wolfson Building
Christ's Pieces
Christ's College
Senate House
Great St Mary's Church
Market
King's College Chapel
St Bene't's Church
Emmanuel College
Pembroke College
Peterhouse
Downing College
A603
Fitzwilliam Museum
A1307
Scott Polar Research Institute

N

0   Miles   1
0   Kilometres   1

Cambridge. EH

Cambridge, St John's College Library, the River Cam and the Bridge of Sighs. JB

neo-classical college buildings are found at Downing, an early 19th-century college in the Greek Revival style, by William Wilkins.

Wilkins was equally at home with the Gothic Revival. In the 1820s he designed the splendid gatehouse and screen for King's College. At the same time St John's College acquired in Rickman's New Court some bold, romantic, 'pasteboard' Gothic. In the 1860s G G Scott gave St John's a new Chapel with a huge Early English style tower. In Cambridge itself, in the same years G F Bodley designed All Saints Church, Jesus Lane, a beautiful and original reinterpretation of English Decorated, and not mere copyism. The interior has pre-Raphaelite decoration by William Morris. The late 19th century produced exotic hybrids in Cambridge as elsewhere. Newnham College, begun in the 1870s, has a charmingly lopsided gate-tower and exudes all the 'sweetness and light' of the Queen Anne style. In the 1880s Selwyn College was built in decorative neo-Tudor. Amongst Cambridge's theological colleges, Westminster is notable for its freely-mixed Tudor and 17th-century motifs and its weird, squashed tower.

There is much 20th-century work in Cambridge and a few glimpses must suffice. During the 1920s and 1930s G G Scott designed the new University Library, with its dominant tower and careful massing. Opposite, he designed the neo-Georgian Memorial Court for Clare College. The Polar Research Institute in Lensfield Road is a little 1930s gem and St John's Chapel Court is as redolent of 1940 as Walton's 'Spitfire Prelude'. In the 1960s came New Hall, with a Pop Art dome and feminine white brick, and concrete. Concrete was used more glamorously in the Cripps Building at St John's, of 1963–7, which is a modern addition of real quality. The Faculty of History Library, finished as long ago as 1968, remains controversial and fascinating. Trinity College's Wolfson Building of 1968–72, a liner stranded behind hairdressers' and bookshops, can only really be seen from the top of Great St Mary's Tower, but is worth the climb. In the 1970s Robinson College, a scholar's brick fortress shutting out an uncivilized world, was built. Its chapel has stained glass by John Piper. Newnham's blank-faced, toy-like stack for rare books was built in 1981–2 and Fitzwilliam College was

given an interesting new chapel in the early 1990s.

The best way to see Cambridge is from the river; by punt from Jesus Green, along the academic Elysium of The Backs where college gardens edge the water on one side with meadows and trees on the other. There is plenty here to beguile the eye in this most famous of English landscapes. St John's dominates the top end of this idyllic scenery, its Bridge of Sighs closing the view. Below, an oriel windows dips romantically into the water. The river meanders past Trinity Library to Clare's luxuriant terraces and the wide open lawns of King's College – a scene as familiar as St Mark's in Venice. Weeping willows foil a succession of stone bridges, creating vistas and sudden, unexpected views of grazing cattle, lichened stone and impeccably kept grass; English 'sharawaggi' at its finest. Alleys, courts and gardens find their way to the river; buildings drift by like perspective sculptures; river-washed cobbles give way to gleaming towers and pinnacles. It is possible to go on beneath the willow-pattern Mathematical Bridge at Queen's to the shady reaches of Granchester Meadows. Or else there is the leisurely turn-around with everything seen again, but differently. For those who float along The Backs to look at Cambridge there is this exquisite advice – do not hurry.

94
King's Lynn, Norfolk

TF 618200. 12 miles (19.3 km) NE of Wisbech, on A47

Defoe described the cultured and cosmopolitan seaport of King's Lynn in the 1720s as 'a beautiful, well built and well situated town' of 'more gentry and gaiety' than Norwich (97, N) or Great Yarmouth (N). Closer in spirit and development to Harwich than either of these two, King's Lynn had barely existed before the Conquest, but was promoted by the Bishops of Norwich in the 12th century to take advantage of its natural site. Its history is reflected in its physical form, a planned grid street pattern enclosed by walls on the landward side. Saturday Market Place is the ancient core, and the town was soon extended northwards by the foundation of Tuesday Market Place, the two centres being united under the name of Bishops Lynn in 1204. Henry VIII changed its name to King's Lynn.

By the 13th century it was already one of the busiest ports in the country, rivalling its Lincolnshire neighbour Boston as a centre of international trade. It had close ties with North Germany and the Baltic, importing furs, fish and timber, as well as wine from Gascony, Cordovan leather and raisins, dates and figs from Spain. But it was not isolated from the rest of the country by the Fen hinterland – the Great Ouse and its tributaries were a teeming highway until the coming of the railways. St Ives (C), with its celebrated annual wool fair, passed its trade through Lynn but as the German Hansa gradually monopolised the wool trade, grain became the foremost export.

Naturally, the river was the focus of attention in this town devoted to trade. King Street, which prior to reclamation formed the river frontage, is now largely Georgian, but holds one surprise in a timber-framed structure dating from the 12th century. Reclamation provided more land for the wealthy merchants' houses which are characterised by long narrow plots of land, with yards and warehouses running down to private quays. Clifton House in Queen Street is one of the best . Its smart brick front of 1708 with barley-sugar columns conceals the remnants of a medieval house with vaulted undercroft and rare tile pavement. In the rear yard stands a tall brick Elizabethan look-out tower commanding a wide prospect over the roofs of the warehouses to the river. Nelson Street has fine timber-framed houses including Hampton Court and some Georgian brick. The 'Greenland Fisheries', Bridge Street, with its oriel windows, was built by the merchant John Atkin in 1605. A remarkable collection of early warehouses includes the timber-framed Hanseatic Warehouse in St Margarets Lane and a good 16th–17th century group in Kings Staithe Lane.

King's Lynn, Custom House. RCHME

Lynn's churches have nothing to rival the Boston Stump in height, but St Margaret's Church, Saturday Market, was built to a huge scale with a twin-towered west front. The Red Mount Chapel, The Walk, of 1485, built as a wayside chapel for Walsingham pilgrims, has a miniature fan vault by John Wastell. Lynn boasts two Guildhalls, Holy Trinity of 1421 with its chequerboard flushwork, facing Saturday Market, and St George, c.1406

in King Street, used as a theatre in Elizabeth I's time, and now, appropriately, the Fermoy Centre and home of the Arts Festival.

The spacious Tuesday Market with its Georgian houses was once presided over by a domed octagonal market cross built by Henry Bell, amateur architect and sometime mayor of the town. His Duke's Head now takes pride of place, built for Sir John Turner to accommodate visitors to the Merchants' Exchange of

1683. This sophisticated little building on Purfleet Quay was Bell's masterpiece. A perfect stone box, it is crowned by a cupola and adorned with an utterly camp statue of Charles II. It soon became the Custom House and the arcaded ground floor was enclosed. After nearly 300 years, Customs left the building in 1990, and it stands empty, its future uncertain.

95

Lavenham, Suffolk

TL 915494. On A1141, 10½ miles (16.8 km) SE of Bury St Edmunds

Thomas Spring, 'The Rich Clothier' of Lavenham, was the wealthiest commoner in England, outside London, in 1524 and Lavenham the fourteenth richest town in the land, above county towns such as York and Lincoln. Spring, like the rest of the townspeople, owed his prosperity to the production of woollen cloth. A cottage industry, it left no legacy of mills or other purpose-built structures, but a remarkable collection of timber-framed medieval merchants' houses and one of the most magnificent parish churches in England.

This peak of prosperity took expression in the lavish rebuilding of the church of St Peter and St Paul, perhaps by the architect John Wastell. Bequests show that the whole community played a part, but a good deal of the money was contributed by the top clothier families. The Earl of Oxford's boar and mullet

Lavenham, Little Hall. JC

(star) emblems are rivalled by Spring's initials and merchant's mark, and by the coat of arms he acquired shortly before his death. The timber screen of his tomb, at the east end of the north aisle, is a piece of woodcarving of astonishing virtuosity, notably surpassing that of the 13th earl in the south aisle.

The merchants' houses which date from this period are the embodiment of ostentatious display. Timber was used lavishly, with the vertical wall studs closely spaced for maximum effect, carved bressumers and corner posts, and elaborate oriel windows. Inside, the heavily moulded beams and the wall surfaces were painted or hung with rich fabrics.

The best starting place to view Lavenham is the Market Place. It is worth acquiring a copy of the informative *A walk around Lavenham* published by the Suffolk Preservation Society, whose headquarters, Little Hall, is open to the public. Restored in 1924, this is a typical medieval open hall-house with a fine crown post roof. Medieval shopfronts survive in several houses, the best preserved with shutters which could be propped to form a counter, in what is now the Tourist Information Centre. The opulent Corpus Christi Guildhall, dating from around 1520, was restored in the 1920s and is now owned by the National Trust.

Ironically, the survival of so much of medieval Lavenham was the result of the town's profound economic decline from the later part of the 16th century. Complete Georgian buildings are in short supply although there are one or two re-frontings in brick, notably the fine Firs House in Church Street. More often houses were modernised with the insertion of casement or sash windows. Many were subdivided into tenements, and gradually fell into disrepair. The Guildhall itself was turned into a workhouse for 80 paupers.

By the beginning of the 19th century, demolition was rife and two of the guildhalls were lost as late as the last quarter of the century. But by this time Lavenham's fortunes as an industrial centre were reviving with expansion of the horsehair business, and the preservation movement was gaining

momentum. The Guildhall of Our Lady, which had become the Wool Hall after the Reformation, was in 1911 saved from a similar fate by public outcry and the support of the Society for the Preservation of Ancient Buildings. Its frame was re-erected and now forms part of the Swan Hotel. From the 1920s this new-found enthusiasm gave rise to a wave of restoration, plaster stripping and reinstatement of medieval features, which is responsible for the appearance of the town today.

96

Letchworth, Hertfordshire

TL 221325. At junction 9, A1(M), 5 miles (8 km) N of Stevenage

Garden Cities of Tomorrow was a book with a new vision of England. Its author, Ebenezer Howard, shorthand clerk, free-thinker and persuasive writer, described how Garden Cities could be built to replace squalid towns and outlined a new urban way of life. All kinds of people would live and work together in congenial surroundings, industry would be zoned away on the outskirts and the whole place would be encircled by farmland and countryside: a city in a garden.

In 1903 Howard's vision was turned into reality when Letchworth, England's First Garden City, was launched. It was a privately financed venture and often short of capital, but it grew to be successful and influential both at home and abroad. Its architects were Parker and Unwin, Arts and Crafts men who wore tweed suits, were related by marriage, and vegetarian. They gave Letchworth much of its shape and style; their flexibility as planners allowed the Garden City to emerge as a pleasing mix of formal and informal spaces and buildings.

The centre was planned along baroque lines, with radiating avenues lined with trees. The main street, Broadway, has the Town Hall and former grammar school along one side. These are in the neo-Georgian style like many of the nearby shops and offices. Some of it is very convincing. And already there

Letchworth, Rusby Mead. JB

are trees, shrubs and gardens shouldering their way into town. Picturesque, symmetrical groups of houses ramble away from the shops, the lush vegetation takes over, and the contrived views, incidents and details of an English Arcadia begin. Everywhere there are mature, deciduous trees (grown tall since Howard's time), glimpses of parks, gentle twists and turns, and cul-de-sacs, with gleaming red pillar-boxes.

In addition to those buildings of Parker and Unwin, many houses in this picture-book townscape were designed by budding young architects, among them Oswald P Milne, Geoffry Lucas, Robert Bennett and M H Baillie-Scott. Clever use was made of vernacular scale and materials, with brick, tiles, roughcast, weatherboarding, and black, white and green paint much in evidence. Arunside (now a museum), Dents Cottage, Hallbarn and Tanglewood are individual houses of note. W H Cowlishaw's The Cloisters is a weird pile of 1906–8. Good work can be found in Jackmans Place, Ridge Road and Nevells Road, where several examples survive from the 1905 Cheap Cottages Exhibition. Despite the cottages, Letchworth was an industrial town although its industry was banished beyond the railway line and even here care was taken in choosing the right materials and in landscaping sites. The Spirella Factory of 1912–22 still dominates the area with its castle-like presence.

Letchworth has grown larger than was ever intended, but its essential character and atmosphere remain intact. It established standards for

relaxed, low-density living which owed much to Ebenezer Howard's philanthropy and something to English traditions of Picturesque planning and Model Villages. Letchworth's stated intention was to deliver to its residents 'a full measure of social life', a laudable aim which led on to the more conventional Welwyn Garden City (H), produced delightful spin-offs like Hampstead Garden Suburb and ultimately paved the way to England's New Towns and to Milton Keynes in Buckinghamshire.

97
Norwich, Norfolk

TG 232085.

Norwich was a great medieval city. Already populous by the Conquest, it reached its heyday as a cloth town and port in the late Middle Ages and in the 1520s was the richest provincial town in the country. An influx of skilled refugee clothmakers from religious persecution in Holland and France buffered it from the long-term effects of the subsequent recession, which devastated its lesser rivals. By 1579 there were approximately 6,000 of these 'Strangers' out of a population of c.16,000. By 1700, Norwich had grown to be the largest town outside of London, although soon to be outstripped by Bristol. Visiting in 1722, Defoe wrote: 'If a stranger were to ride through or view the city of Norwich for a day, he would have reason to think that here was a town without inhabitants; but on the contrary, if he was to view the city, either on a Sabbath day or any public occasion, he would wonder where all the people could dwell, the multitude is so great. But the case is this; the inhabitants being all busy at their manufacture, dwell in their combing shops, twisting mills and other work houses.'

Thetford rivalled Norwich during the Saxon period, but Norwich gained the upper hand, and the cathedral, after the Conquest. The building of the Castle, sweeping away 100 houses, shifted the focus from the Saxon market place at Tombland to the new one at Mancroft.

(Twentieth-century disruption on a similar scale has seen the excavation of a very large hole in the ground near the Castle to accommodate a shopping mall.) Today Mancroft remains the heart of the city, as the site of the largest open-air market place in England. The principal town church of St Peter Mancroft (1430–55) faces the much restored medieval Guildhall across a sea of awnings, presided over by the Swedish-style City Hall (1932–8) by C H James and S R Pierce which Pevsner described as 'the foremost English public building between the wars'.

The bewildering labyrinth of streets, most picturesque of which is Elm Hill, forming the medieval centre was confined between the River Wensum and the 2¼ mile (3.6 km) circuit of walls. Impressive remains of the largely 14th-century fortifications include the early brick Cow Tower of 1380. The Bishop's Bridge, c.1340, is the only survivor of no less than five medieval bridges. Blackfriars Bridge was rebuilt by Sir John Soane in 1783.

Churches form the lynchpins in the city's fabric. In 1500 Norwich had 50 at least, and there are still 31 although many of them have been put to other uses. Some have Saxon origins, but as a group they are pre-eminently a showcase of the Perpendicular style, especially the late 15th-century St Michael Coslany and St George, both in Colegate, St Andrews in St Andrew Street, and St Stephen in Rampant Horse Street. The largely late 14th-century St Giles, in the street of the same name, has a fine hammerbeam roof and soaring tower. The tiny St Julian in King Street, mostly rebuilt after Second World War bomb damage, contained in its churchyard the anchorage of the 14th-century mystic Dame Julian, authoress of *The Revelations of Divine Love*.

Medieval Norwich had all the usual religious houses, and the city now possesses the only substantially complete friars' church in England. Blackfriars, or St Andrews Hall, in St Andrew Street, with its distinctive plan of nave and chancel separated by a narrow passageway, was bought by the City Council after the Reformation for

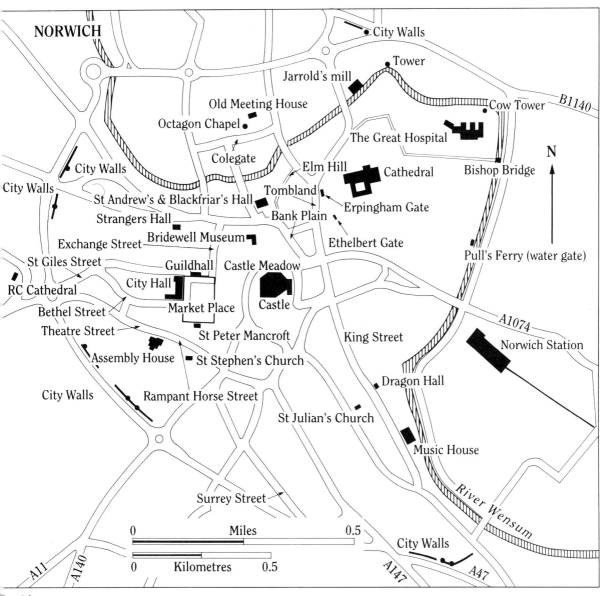

Norwich. EH

s great preaching space made a superb ivic hall. Another remarkable survival the Great Hospital in Bishopgate, ounded in 1249 by Bishop Walter de uffield as a house for decrepit chaplains nd the sick poor. The chancel, rebuilt y Bishop Despenser c.1380, has a onderful ceiling painted with 252 pread eagles, and was later floored over o form the women's wards, lined with ndividual timber cubicles.

A number of the great merchants' houses are accessible. Dragon Hall, formerly The Old Barge Inn, by the river on King Street, is a timber-framed house which has recently been stripped out to reveal a grand first-floor hall. Nearby, behind a 17th-century brick facade, lurks one of the oldest houses in the country, the late 12th-century Music House, with its vaulted undercroft. Hidden beneath its streets, Norwich has

an unparalleled system of medieval undercrofts, many of them brick. Early examples are found at the Bridewell Museum of industry and commerce, Bridewell Alley, better known for its superb knapped flint front, and Strangers Hall, Charing Cross, now a museum of domestic life and one of the best of the merchants' houses from the 15th and 16th centuries. Suckling House, St Andrew Street, now a café, has

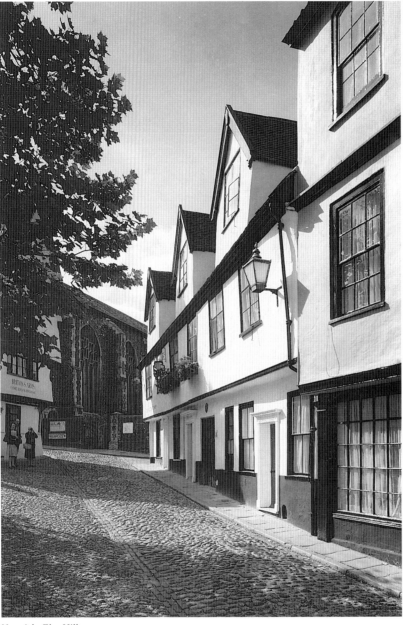

Norwich, Elm Hill. JB

chapels in the county. St Giles is a largely Georgian street, interspersed with some early 20th-century baroque by G J Skipper, the inventive and versatile local architect. Churchman's House, Bethel Street, *c*.1750, now the Registry Office, has exquisite rococo plasterwork and chimney pieces.

The early 19th century was marked by the founding of the Norwich Society of Artists by John Crome. The brilliant watercolourist John Sell Cotman, a native of the city, devoted much of his energies to views catering to the antiquarian tastes of the time, including his *Architectural Antiquities of Norfolk* (1812–18). Diversification of commerce and industry produced the 1834 yarn mill on the river. It now houses Jarrolds the printers, and is the closest thing in Norwich to a 'dark Satanic mill', described by Ian Nairn as 'the noblest of all English Industrial Revolution mills'. Skipper's showpieces are the chunky baroque Norwich Union of 1903–4 in Surrey Street, and, in complete contrast, the delicate Art Nouveau facade of the Royal Arcade in Castle Street. Much more prominent than the Anglican cathedral in the Norwich skyline is the Duke of Norfolk's Roman Catholic St John Baptist (1884–1910), St Giles Gate, now a cathedral, a committed exercise in historicist Early English Gothic by Sir G G and J O Scott.

Norwich became the second university town in the region in 1964, and the University is distinguished by Sir Denys Lasdun's ziggurats, and two generations of work by Foster Associates, the Sainsbury Centre and its recent extension in the form of a semi-subterranean wing behind a crescent wall of glass. The development of the complex is now being co-ordinated with large additions by architect Rick Mather.

98

Somerleyton Village, Suffolk

TM 485975. 5 miles (8 km) NW of Lowestoft, off B1074

Somerleyton is twenty-eight model cottages and a school forming a loose crescent around a green. It was one of

an early 16th-century open hall with a scissor brace and crown post roof and a fine bay window to the courtyard.

The cosmopolitan society of 18th-century Norwich, thriving on the agricultural prosperity of the county, is reflected by the 1754 elegant Assembly Rooms in Theatre Street. The architect

was Thomas Ivory, the founder member of a dynasty of sculptors, joiners and architects that dominated the architectural scene in the city. The Octagon Chapel (1754–6) in Colegate was his, which together with its neighbouring Old Meeting House (1693), are the best Nonconformist

he most successful versions of John
Nash's famous Picturesque village of
Blaise Hamlet near Bristol, built in
1810. Somerleyton dates back to c.1850
and was designed by John Thomas, a
sculptor who dabbled in architecture,
for Sir Morton Peto, business magnate,
MP and railway builder. Peto also got
Thomas to build Somerleyton Hall, in
exuberant neo-Jacobean, and St Mary's
church in flint-and-stone Gothic.

The Model Village is on a typically
flat, edge-of-Broadland site. The
cottages housed Peto's estate workers
and were built in a mixed Old English
style. They were described as being
'Substantial' and 'Highly Ornamental'
and offering, 'a singular and rare
attention to the comfort and morality of
Peasant Families'. In other words, they
were coarsely decorated and had more
bedrooms than usual. Built of brick,
they have sham half-timbering, porches,
tall chimneys (recommended by Nash)
and plenty of thatch. The plum and
cream-coloured woodwork is
appropriately reminiscent of Victorian

railway carriages. Windows and
doorways are picked out in white paint.
Each house is different to its neighbour
and each has a garden and an
uninterrupted view. At the back there
are fields. The school is especially
ornate, with elaborate chimneys and
chinoiserie-latticed windows.

Somerleyton is an easygoing, open-
ended place, but it wears a blank smile
these days. The green needs people to
decorate it, to add life and movement;
like sheep in a park or pheasants in a
wood. That was an important part of
Picturesque planning theory. Smoking
chimneystacks, the sounds of a horse
and cart or of wood being chopped were
also highly desirable effects. But the late
20th century does not want to play.
Down the lane it makes a half-hearted
attempt with its own kind of developer's
picturesque. After that it gives up.

Somerleyton still has a real country
railway station, with red and white
signals, bramble-fringed platforms, and
an unkempt station house. A strange
entrée to a strange village.

99
Southwold, Suffolk

TM 508763. On coast, 8 miles
(12.8 km) E of Halesworth, on
A1095

A seaside town, domestic-scaled, gentle
and genteel. Until the River Blyth silted
up, Southwold was a port, famous for
boat-building, red sprats and the Battle
of Sole Bay (1672). The main industry in
the town today is brewing.

Medieval Southwold was wrecked by
a fire in 1659 and the town was re-
shaped around the sea-front and a series
of gaps and greens created by the blaze.
Streets are narrow and lined by
characterful shops, houses and matey-
looking pubs. The greens provide a real
sense of locality, their openness
contrasting enjoyably with the closure of
the streets and lanes. Incidents are
created by the buildings themselves:
shades of pink, blue and white splashed
here and there, boldly shaped bow
windows, sign-writing with a nautical
flavour, flint cobble walls.

The most interesting part of
Southwold forms a wedge between Gun
Hill and Church Green. The early 19th-
century fashion for 'sea air' and
'watering' brought well-proportioned
marine villas and lodging houses to
South Green and the cliffs along the
front. Regency House, 1828, is one of
the best, with a swelling bow front and
painted window shutters. Centre Cliff is
a pleasant speculative row of 1829 with a
stuccoed middle. At its far end a later
wing bulges with rich ironwork. This is
flush with the sea-front. A strip of
bleached promenade, a change of level
and there is the beach; grey-blue pebbles
surging round a line of multicoloured
bathing huts. Beyond Longisland Cliff
more down-to-earth houses take over;
red and white brick terraces with
wooden verandahs. In the streets behind
North Parade lies Victorian Southwold.
St James' Green leads back inland, to
Stradbroke Road and Sole Bay Inn (a
pub from a Rowlandson print) on the
corner. Almost opposite stands a
lighthouse, a plain white cylinder rising
above a black tarred wall: in these blunt

Somerleyton. JC

113

100
Stewartby, Bedfordshire

TL 023423. 3 miles (4.8 km) N of Ampthill, off B530

Southwold, the lighthouse. JSC

Stewartby is brick. It was built as an estate village by the London Brick Company from 1927 onwards and its workers and pensioners are housed here beneath the tall chimneystacks of the works. Stewartby bricks are reddish-brown wirecuts, some with textured faces. Almost everything that can be is made of brick; houses and sheds, walls and pavements, school and public buildings. The railway station still has low, brick-paved platforms.

At Stewartby's centre is a large green with houses and other buildings around it. The Village Hall is a stark neo-Colonial building, with a large wooden pediment and a clock turret. It was designed, along with the Club, by E V Harris. The Secondary Modern School, with main block topped by another clock turret, was by O P Milne.

Housing is set back from the streets, with communal areas of grass in front and private gardens behind. Most of it consists of semi-detached pairs with clay tile roofs, white painted doors and windows and almost no decoration; just an occasional string course or two.

These houses are made in the same style as much early council housing; decent, austere, oddly evocative of washing lines, boiled cabbage and British war films. On the far side of the green is a mid-1950s estate of old people's homes. These are by Richardson and Houfe and very much in the almshouse tradition: rows of neo-

forms set back a few yards from the sea is all the vigour of the nautical style. A sailor's touch is added by the painted figurehead mounted on a wall nearby. There used to be others scattered around the town; exotic symbols of ships and the sea, and faraway places.

East and Church Greens are a rough-and-ready mix of Adnams Brewery buildings and dog-eared cottages in faded ice-cream colours. Salt-water and malt smells sharpen the air. The brewery is Victorian, and so is the over-restoration of St Edmund's Church a few yards further on. Fine flushwork and a huge tower. Beautiful early woodwork

inside, especially the chancel screen and choir stalls; on one a medieval wretch pulls a face with his finger in his mouth. Bartholomew Green and Bank Alley lead back to the High Street and Market Place, the centre of Southwold with Town Hall, town pump, hotels and shops.

Southwold has kept its identity intact. There is an absence of tourist tat and seaside bric-a-brac. Instead there are chummy buildings, odd corners and ship-shape Greens, back-street pubs and colourful beer bottle labels: all as fresh as the East wind that scours the Suffolk coast.

Stewartby. BCC

114

eorgian single-storey cottages with
rominent chimneys, sash windows and
ather grand front doors. The layout is
ormal and collegiate with a Hall placed
t the end of a tree-lined avenue and the
ottages grouped around grassed and
aved quadrangles. The swept roof of the
Iall, the regularly placed lanterns and
herry blossoms lend a faintly surreal
uality to these streets which are
ncluttered by passers-by or motor
ehicles.

Stewartby is a strangely deserted
lace; a black-and-white image of
ngland with simple houses and a
ackcloth of quietly smoking chimneys.

101

tour Valley, Essex–Suffolk Border

Stour watermeadows. JB

associate my careless boyhood with all
hat lies on the banks of the Stour.
hose scenes made me a painter.' No
ther English painter is so inextricably
nked with a certain landscape than is
ohn Constable with the Stour Valley.
very summer tourists come in their
housands to seek 'Constable Country'.
Iost congregate at Flatford (S), with its
eassuringly familiar images of the Mill
nd Willy Lot's cottage, and then pay a
isit to Dedham (E). But it is worth
enturing a little further in order to
ppreciate 'its well cultivated uplands,
ts woods and rivers, with numerous
cattered villages and churches, farms
nd picturesque cottages'.

This was a cloth-producing area in
he 15th and 16th centuries, not quite in
he same league as Lavenham (95, S)
ut prosperous enough to produce a
umber of very fine churches and
ubstantial clothiers' houses. Stratford
t Mary Church, once on the main road
o London, has a north aisle like a
illboard, advertising the names of its
atrons, and an alphabet flushwork to
emind travellers of their devotions. The
mart jettied Weavers House at the other
nd of the village had a workshop fitted
ut with looms.

Further up the valley, the soaring
ower of the church of Stoke by Nayland
orms a prominent landmark. Two
ouses to the west of the church make a

lavish display of close-studding. Most are
more reticent, a coat of colourwashed
plaster being the traditional finish.

Constable's birthplace, East Bergholt
(S), is a large village, strung out around
the old heath, following the contour of
the north bank of the Stour. It is typical
of this part of Suffolk in its varied
character of timber-framed medieval
open-hall houses, rendered cottages and
smart white brick villas. The house of
Constable's father was one of a group of
handsome red brick mansions around
the church. Demolished in the 1840s, its
place is now marked only by the railings
and converted stable block. John's
studio, Moss Cottage in Cemetery Lane,
has been preserved. The church tower,
intended to outdo Dedham, was started
in 1525, but expensive rebuilding of the
body of the church was still in train
twenty years later, after which it ran out
of steam, leaving the tower an
unfinished stump. The bells are housed
in a timber bellcage on the ground.

Much more cosmopolitan than
Bergholt in Constable's time were
Dedham and Mistley (E). Dedham's
main street is lined with elegant red and
gault brick facades behind which
medieval houses hide, revealed only by
their steep tiled roofs and huge stacks.
Shermans is the ultimate in chic cheek,
its exquisite baroque facade as thin as a
piece of stage scenery. It is probably by
the same hand as built the former

grammar school of 1732 opposite and
which Constable attended as a boy.
Raymond Erith's Frog End is an
accomplished development of houses in
the vernacular idiom, fitting in well with
the village scene; his Great House (1936)
in the High Street is a chaste piece in
white brick.

Mistley was the Stour port from
which Constable's father transported his
corn to London aboard his ship, *The
Telegraph*. Remarkable as it seems
today, during the same period Richard
Rigby, MP, of Mistley Hall was
attempting to transform the town into a
fashionable spa, employing as his
architect Robert Adam. Very little of his
work survives, save a pedimented row of
cottages in the square with its swan
fountain and the extraordinary paired
towers of the otherwise demolished
church. It is rather the industrial
character of the town which remains
strong, dominated by the looming forms
of 19th-century maltings, and a rich
malty aroma still hangs in the air.

102

Wisbech, Cambridgeshire

TF 465095. 12 miles (19.3 km) SW
of King's Lynn, on A47

Wisbech used to be a flourishing market
and river port. It grew on the banks of

Wisbech, North Brink. JB

the River Nene to which it owed its prosperity and its character. In the 18th and 19th centuries it was a centre for trading and shipping corn and agricultural produce. At its heart lay the river, and along the riverside two startling streets of buildings were created; North Brink and South Brink.

The Brinks, like The Backs in Cambridge, are unique. Two curving cliffs of houses, old granaries, stables, hotels and public buildings all thrown together. North Brink is the more vivid; almost everything here is worth a look. A few 'snapshots' must do, beginning near Wisbech bridge (a vulgar 1930s design) with the pedimented Town Hall and an ebullient Edwardian bank. Then a run of smart Georgian houses, one with wavy bay windows, a humble warehouse, Peckover House and an eye-jolting gabled row. Then plainer houses and detached villas sweeping round to Elgood's Brewery; unfussy, early industrial buildings and still brewing beer. North Brink's (and Wisbech's) smartest building is Peckover House, built in the 1720s. Inside there is rich rococo craftsmanship and a staircase with plaster decoration of an elegant

marine kind. At the back there are luxuriant gardens.

South Brink's buildings are less exciting, more in-and-out and shabby-genteel. There is a faded hotel, a Sessions House with tall windows, one or two rude interlopers, and an early 19th-century terrace with pleasingly spare details. On both Brinks, brick is the main material; brick in various shades of brown, red and yellow, giving flat, light-reflecting fronts which go well with the Fens.

In the port's heyday there were great storehouses, boat-building yards, and another brewery below the bridge. Ships rode high between the Brinks, the clutter of tall masts and rigging lending energy and meaning to this river town. The ships have gone; a spiritual gap in the townscape remains. Gone too is the Wisbech Canal, the railway, and the Tramway, a wonderfully slow passenger-and-fruit carrying service which ran between Wisbech and Upwell (N). Down on Nene Quay several collapsing or converted warehouses remain, but the great quayside ranges seen in old photographs have been pulled down.

North of the bridge is the deserted,

triangular Old Market with solid-looking houses and interesting fanlights. Back across the river, past the prickly Clarkson Memorial, lies the Market Square, a long rectangle with dull shop fronts and a large late 18th-century hotel at one end. An unobtrusive street on the south side leads through to Union Place, a planned piece of townscape with ordered Georgian terraces laid out round a garden on the site of Wisbech Castle. The sharp contrast between this secluded oval and the bustle of Market Square or the long vistas of the Brinks was surely intentional. Museum Square was a part of the development. The Museum has Greek Revival details and an interior of dark polished wood and glass cabinets. Steps lead down from the small square to the medieval church of SS Peter and Paul: two saints, two naves two aisles, and a big tower.

Wisbech's different but well-related spaces, its robust Georgian buildings, riverscape and Brinks make it an important provincial survivor. The plainness and lack of fuss in its streets and houses are echoed in the empty fields and orchards that lie all around this haunting marshland town.

116

Bibliography

D Alderton and J Booker, *The Batsford Guide to the Industrial Archaeology of East Anglia*, Batsford, 1980.

F Bond, *The Cathedrals of England and Wales*, 1912.

R Bruce-Mitford, *The Sutton Hoo Ship Burial*, British Museum, 3rd edn 1979.

H M Cautley, *Norfolk Churches*, Boydell Press, 4th edn, rev. 1975.

H M Cautley, *Suffolk Churches*, Boydell Press, 4th edn, rev. 1975.

G Darley, *Villages of Vision*, Architectural Press, 1975.

D Gareth Davies and C Saunders, *Verulamium*, City and District of St Albans, 1986.

D Defoe, *A Tour Through The Whole Island of Great Britain* Penguin, 1971 (first published 1724–6).

D Dymond and E Martin (eds), *An Historical Atlas of Suffolk*, Suffolk County Council Planning Dept and Suffolk Institute of Archaeology and History, 1988.

C Fiennes, *The Journeys of Celia Fiennes*, Macdonald and Co., 1983.

B Gulloway, *A History of Cambridgeshire*, Phillimore, 1983.

R M Healey, *Hertfordshire: A Shell Guide*, Faber & Faber, 1982.

C A Hewett, *Church Carpentry*, Phillimore, 1982.

C McKean, *Architectural Guide to Cambridge and East Anglia since 1920*, RIBA, 1982.

M Miller, *Letchworth*, Phillimore, 1989.

B Oliver, *Old Houses and Village Buildings in East Anglia*, 1912.

N Pevsner, The Buildings of England: *Bedfordshire and the County of Huntingdon and Peterborough; Cambridgeshire; Essex* (2nd edn, rev. by Enid Radcliffe); *Hertfordshire* (2nd edn, rev. by Bridget Cherry); *North-East Norfolk and Norwich; North-west and South Norfolk; Suffolk* (2nd edn, rev. by Enid Radcliffe). Penguin, various editions and dates.

N Pevsner and P Metcalf, *The Cathedrals of England*, Penguin, 1985.

F Pryor, *Flag Fen*, Batsford and English Heritage, 1991.

Victoria County History of Essex, Vols I–VIII, 1903–83.

P Wade-Martins (ed) and D A Edwards, *Norfolk from the Air*, Norfolk Museums Service, 1987.

S Wade-Martins, *A History of Norfolk*, Phillimore, 1984.

F Woodman, *The Architectural History of King's College Chapel*, Routledge & Kegan Paul, 1986.

Index

Note: gazetteer entries are listed in **bold**, by their *page* number

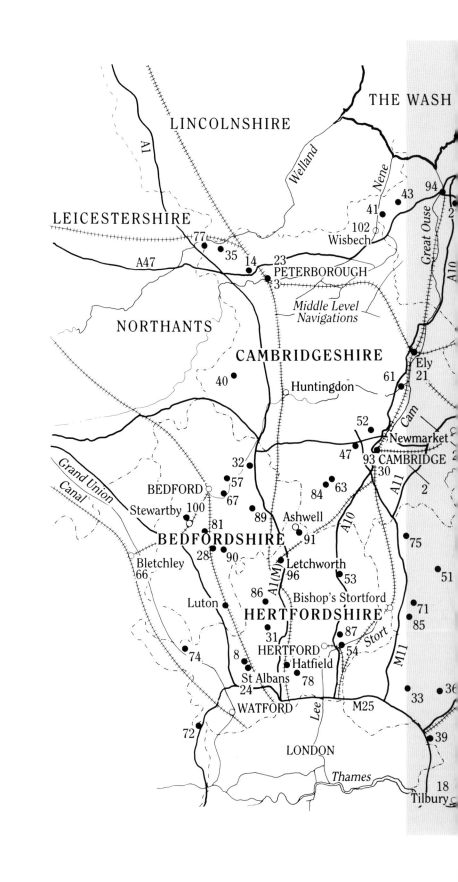